T0129182

THE ONLY
CAT BOOK
YOU'LL EVER NEED

The Essentials for Staying
One Step Ahead of Your Feline

Steve Duno

Edited by Andrea Mattei

Adams Media
New York London Toronto Sydney New Delhi

Aadamsmedia

Adams Media
An Imprint of Simon & Schuster, Inc.
57 Littlefield Street
Avon, Massachusetts 02322

For information about special discounts for bulk purchases, please contact Simon & Schuster Special Sales at 1-866-506-1949 or business@simonandschuster.com.

The Simon & Schuster Speakers Bureau can bring authors to your live event. For more information or to book an event contact the Simon & Schuster Speakers Bureau at 1-866-248-3049 or visit our website at www.simonspeakers.com.

Manufactured in the United States of America

Contains portions of material adapted and abridged from
The Everything® Cat Book by Steve Duno, © 1997, Simon & Schuster, Inc.

Library of Congress Cataloging-in-Publication Data
Duno, Steve.
The only cat book you'll ever need / By Steve Duno.
p.   cm.
ISBN 1-59337-288-4
1. Cats. I. Title.

SF447.D865 2005
636.8--dc22

2005007432

ISBN 978-1-59337-288-0

Contents

Chapter 8: Teaching Basic Behaviors • 73

Chapter 9: Troubleshooting Behavior Problems • 84

Chapter 10: Kitty Health Care and First Aid • 106

Chapter 11: Common Illnesses and Health Problems • 131

Appendix: Cat Associations and Organizations • 175

Index • 177

Acknowledgments

Special thanks to Debra M. Eldredge, D.V.M., for sharing her veterinary knowledge and expertise regarding the medical information presented in this book.

Introduction

*C*ats are amazing creatures. They leap from tables to counter-tops with the ease of acrobats. They happily hide in spaces no dog—or human—could ever imagine squeezing into. Their reflexes are faster than lightning. Though far smaller than their wild relations, the domestic feline is no less fascinating and awe inspiring. She's also quite adept at getting her way. Ask any kitty parent, and he'll tell you that his tabby has him totally wrapped around her tiny paw.

Perhaps we cat lovers are enraptured by our beguiling felines because they can be so mysterious and intriguing. Unlike loyal, loving canines, who wear their hearts on their sleeves, cats can be harder to read. And so, we long to know what makes them tick.

Though they most likely adore their humans every bit as much as dogs do, they won't always reveal it. And then there are those times when they do show you just how much they love you. And when they cuddle up next to you, looking up at you with their big, adoring eyes, they just melt your heart.

At times, cats can be ironic little bundles, indeed. People who don't have cats like to think that cats are aloof, manipulative, and self-serving. Nothing could be farther from the truth. To be sure, cats can sometimes be standoffish. But that's on account of their natural reserve and shyness, *not* out of pure dislike or spite. Likewise, although cats are self-sufficient, independent creatures who know how to fend for themselves, that doesn't mean they're unaffectionate loners. This simply proves that cats have continued to reside with human families for thousands of years not out of necessity, but out of *choice*.

Yes, cats certainly are full of surprising paradoxes and incon-sistencies. In many ways, however, cats need not be a total mystery.

Maybe you're already a kitty parent and, at times, you're daunted or perplexed by the hows and whys of your cat's behavior. Or perhaps you're a novice who's thinking about bringing a feline into your fold for the first time. Either way, don't sweat it. You simply need to learn how to think like your cat. What motivates her? How do you meet her needs? What is it about her unique feline psyche and physiology that makes her do the things she does?

Enter *The Only Cat Book You'll Ever Need*. Think of this compact volume as your crash course in all things cat related. In these pages, you'll learn everything from the benefits of choosing a cat for a pet, to any feline maladies you might encounter. So don't believe all the old wives' tales and stereotypes you've heard before. An animal as complex and regal as the domestic feline cannot be reduced to such simple terms. Turn the page, take a peek, and get the story straight for yourself.

Where Do House Cats Come From?

Domestic cats have a long and illustrious history that dates back millions of years. They stalk, leap, hunt, and raise young now in much the same way that they did at the dawn of human civilization, with an ease and skill never lost through all their years of camaraderie with humans. This ancient species is one of the most versatile members of the animal kingdom, easily adjusting to change and content to make the best of any situation. Cats are elegant survivors, and, though fond of their human families, they certainly do not depend on us the way most other pets do. How did cats' forebears evolve? How, exactly, did the domestication of cats occur? And how do domestic cats compare to wild cats?

PREHISTORIC PREDILECTIONS

The domestic cat's forebears and our own primate ancestors both developed at roughly the same time in history, specifically the Eocene age, about fifty million years ago. All mammals owe a debt of gratitude to the demise of the dinosaurs. Had dinosaurs survived and flourished, there would have been no room for all but the tiniest of mammals.

Cats, particularly today's lions and tigers, conveniently became the world's most capable carnivores by default, it seems. The infamous saber-toothed tiger, surely able to take down a giant woolly mammoth, wouldn't have had a chance to evolve if *Tyrannosaurus rex* or *Velociraptor* had survived. The extinction of the dinosaurs made way for mammals, giving primates and cats a chance to flourish and, ultimately, come together in friendship.

Feline fossils dating back to the Pliocene age, approximately twelve to two and one-half million years ago, show many similarities to today's cats. Domestic kitties have, it seems, been doing their thing successfully for quite some time—certainly longer than we have. And, unlike other domesticated animals, like horses or dogs, domestication has not significantly changed cats' anatomical and behavioral attributes.

A MEETING OF THE MINDS: FELINE DOMESTICATION

Cats and humans did not begin their relationship in earnest until we as a society discovered the benefits of agriculture. With the development of agriculture, humans found a way of reliably feeding larger groups of people in comparatively smaller areas. Our nomadic days could finally come to an end, and we could stay in one spot and build cities, schools, and economies.

Mesopotamian and Egyptian cultures became so proficient at farming that they were able to amass surpluses of grain to be stored and used during times of emergency, or simply to be traded for profit. While agricultural success benefited these societies tremendously, they began to experience a common problem: Rodents regularly raided grain storage areas. These little pests not only depleted the grain, they also spread dangerous diseases. And so the ancient cultures enlisted the cat, nature's most efficient rodent controller, to help reduce or eliminate these pests. Here, then, was the genesis of the so-called "domestication" of the cat.

During ancient times, the African wildcat was fairly common in North Africa. In all likelihood, this is the species that the Mesopotamians and Egyptians enlisted for help with rodent problems. A bit larger than today's house cat, these animals took to domestication fairly well and drastically reduced the vermin population in and around granaries and living areas. A feline of similar size also existed in Europe; this ancient European wildcat, probably comparable to today's *Felis sylvestris*, was shyer and fiercer than its African cousin. This cat did not take to domestication all that well. The Asian or Pallas's cat, *Felis manul*, may have possibly been domesticated by the ancient Chinese, and probably contributed genetically to the numerous longhaired Asian cat breeds we see today.

Cat Tales: Kept Under Lock and Key

In addition to serving as a ratter for Egyptian farmers, the domestic cat became a revered creature, seemingly identified with Bastet, the Egyptian goddess of fertility and maternity. The Egyptian ruling class also believed that cats held great power with the gods, and looked to certain feline movements and behaviors as predictions of the future. In fact, the Egyptian population so valued cats that their spread out of Egypt was severely restricted for many centuries.

The cat's popularity spread to different regions when Roman, Babylonian, and Phoenician sailors began to bring them aboard ship to combat rodents, transporting them to other areas of the known world. And so, cats made their way through Europe, China, and India, eventually traveling to Japan. Once the African wildcat made its way to Europe and Asia, it was no doubt interbred with the European wildcat and the Asian wildcat to produce different physical and behavioral qualities. Today's domestic kitty is most likely descended from these animals, though much genetic manipulation has occurred since, resulting in numerous breeds of varying shapes, sizes, weights, and colors.

Gradually, cats became known in all the countries of the world. Then, toward the end of the Roman era and leading into the Middle Ages, cats slowly began to fall into disfavor, predominantly due to the influence of the Roman Catholic Church, which believed in a connection between felines and witchcraft. The idea that cats were the servants of witches and the devil became an all-too-prevalent European belief; popes and commoners alike encouraged the elimination of cats in the name of all that was holy. A sorry turn of events for our small friends, considering how revered and helpful they had been in ancient times. Cats were burned, sacrificed, tortured, and hunted by dogs, who by this time had become man's best friends.

Cat Tales: Size Matters

Currently there are thirty-six different species of wild cats recognized within the family Felidae, and there are many more subspecies within that. Domestic cats are at the lower end of the feline size spectrum—only a dozen or so wild cats are as small as or smaller than our little lap cats. These "petite" cats include the black-footed cat, the flat-headed cat, Geoffrey's cat, the Iriomote cat, the jaguarondi, the marbled cat, the margay, the oncilla, the Pallas's cat, the rusty-spotted cat, the sand cat, and the wildcats.

Fortunately, with the coming of the Black Death in the fourteenth century, the cat's skill at catching rodents began to counter the European population's disdain. Spread by fleas riding on the backs of rats, the plague killed millions of people. And, when one-third of a continent's population is being wiped out, there is little room for petty superstition. At this point, it became clear that any animal who could eliminate a flea-infested, deadly disease-carrying rat was worth his weight in gold.

By the seventeenth century, the cat was generally back in good graces, in part because of increasing artistic respect for feline poise and beauty as well as new appreciation of the animal's cleanliness. These qualities became more respected over time, as discoveries were made about germs and the way disease spreads. Aristocrats and artists alike enjoyed taking cats as their pampered pets, and began to selectively breed them for certain traits, including coat length and overall size.

Spanish, French, and English sailors and settlers brought cats over to the Americas once again primarily as a safeguard against shipboard and granary rodents. Though not as persecuted as in medieval Europe, the cat did suffer somewhat in New England during the brief but dramatic witch-trial period. That faded away, however, and today the cat is as loved and highly respected in the United States as in any other country.

BIG-CAT COUSINS

Though the domestic cats we know and love are not directly related to most of today's wild cats, they do share many behaviors. Maybe, for instance, your little kitty is a fabulous stalker. Guess what? Her stalking instincts are probably almost identical to those of the leopard.

In fact, thinking of domestic cats as miniature leopards in kitty clothing is one of the easiest ways to understand their psyche. Your little tabby's behavior, instincts, and anatomy are much closer to a leopard's than, say, a Chihuahua's are to a wolf or a jackal. That little Chihuahua, if left to his own devices, would not survive for long in the wild. But your sleepy, hospitable kitty would probably do just fine, relying on her close connection to the wilder side of life.

Anatomical and Behavioral Comparisons

All cats belong to the family Felidae, whose members have whiskers, eyes with slit irises, and retractable or semiretractable claws. These animals all hunt prey and eat a primarily meat-based diet. Though their size varies tremendously from species to species (but not from breed to breed), all cats have the same basic anatomy.

Domestic cats have proportionally smaller adrenal glands than their wild cousins; this may enhance their ability to be tamed, for the adrenals produce chemicals that cause an animal to invoke its "fight or flight" survival response. With smaller amounts of these chemicals, our house kitties can be calmer and more tractable.

Because of the enhanced flexibility of the bones connecting the larynx to the skull, lions, tigers, leopards, and jaguars can really roar the house down, so to speak. Aren't you glad that your little feline can't do that, too?

Cat Tales: Long and Short Tails

The domestic cat has a fairly long tail in comparison to its wild brethren. Bobcats and lynxes, for example, have conspicuously short tails. Only cats such as the margay and ocelot have proportionally longer tails than our house cat, probably due to their love of trees. Both species use their long tails to aid in balance, and, in the case of the ocelot, to grab branches for support, much like a monkey.

All cats have the same basic reflex and sense capabilities, though some species, such as the serval, have better hearing than others due to larger outer ears (pinnas or pinnae).

The domestic cat's coat varies in comparison to other species, owing in large part to selective breeding of desired coat traits. A Persian, for example, has a much longer coat than an Abyssinian.

On average, though, a kitty's coat can withstand a very wide range of climates. This wide variation of coat length and patterning is not seen in other cat species. Coat differences among the wild species are only reflections of their differing environments. And although coat thickness and patterning varies widely among wild species, our domestic cat's coat density and patterns are basically now in the hands of breeders, not nature.

As mentioned above, our own feline friends have a hunting style that closely reflects the leopard's and wildcat's stalking and climbing habits. Other cats' hunting habits vary widely. Some species, like the cheetah, use speed and cunning, while others, like the ocelot, capitalize on climbing ability

Cat Tales: Out of the Water!

Although tigers can be at home in the water, not so for domestic felines. Our house cats generally loathe water for anything other than drinking, and they usually avoid it at all costs!

Although local inhabitants routinely tame the African wildcat and caracal, wild felines cannot be tamed the way the domestic cat can. Most other felines are just too wild to make good pets, so don't be tempted to take home any bobcat or puma kittens.

While cats are more solitary animals and do not exhibit the same strong sense of pack mentality as dogs, many house cats will develop strong bonds with each other, particularly if they are litter mates, or if they have been introduced to other cats from a young age. Some cats will even grow attached to their other four-legged family members— yes, even dogs. And yet, domestic kitties often prefer the company of their human companions to that of other cats or animals. This is part of their unique charm, and one of the things that make us love them so much!

Why Choose a Cat?

*A*nyone who is looking to bring a pet into the home has many considerations to weigh carefully. It's not hard to see the advantages that cats and dogs have over other small pets such as turtles, fish, birds, and reptiles. Cats and dogs are far more intelligent, affectionate, and interactive with their human families. These mammals relate the best to people—no wonder they win the hearts of humans more than any of those other creatures. But when it comes down to choosing a cat *or* a dog, there are still several pros and cons to consider.

Although canines are wonderful companions, at the end of the day, there are some distinct advantages to becoming a kitty parent. Following are the top ten reasons for adopting a feline friend.

CATS ARE COMFORTABLE IN SMALL, INDOOR SPACES

According to the American Pet Products Manufacturers Association (APPMA), at the time of the writing of this book, there are approximately 68 million dogs and 73 million cats owned in the United States. For the first time in United States' history, cat owners now outnumber dog owners. One major reason for this trend is increasing urbanization. City life is congested, hurried, and rather unpredictable, all conditions that do not lend well to dog ownership.

When the United States' population was more rurally based, there was plenty of room for dogs to romp, roam, and play, whether on a farm or in a big fenced-in backyard. Life is much less stressful for dogs and humans alike when you can just open the back door, let them outside, and play ball with them in your own yard.

Today, aside from living in more cramped quarters, pet lovers are often single, and spend a lot of time away from home. And there aren't many dogs out there who can make it without going outside for ten or twelve hours at a time.

Apart from the elimination problem, dogs don't enjoy being by themselves for great lengths of time. These highly social creatures are used to the time-honored pack dynamic, and they go stir crazy if they're home alone for too long. Beyond the physical damage bored dogs can wreak, being left alone for too long can also cause dogs a great deal of tension because they feel their human pack members have "abandoned" them. This sort of stress can take its toll on a dog's mental, emotional, and physical health.

Cats, on the other hand, are far more self-sufficient and fare much better when their human families are away from home. Because they are not pack-oriented, cats are instinctively programmed to amuse themselves, and they suffer less from separation anxiety, unlike poor Fido.

CATS ARE LESS COSTLY AND TIME-CONSUMING THAN DOGS

While cats, like dogs, obviously need plenty of care and attention, dogs are higher-maintenance. You need to take dogs out fairly often, they eat much more than cats, they chew through toys and whatever other household items they can get their paws on . . . Dogs can also get really dirty, and unlike their fastidious feline counterparts, they don't give themselves a bath. All in all, dogs require more maintenance than cats, and many people just don't have the time, energy, or money to take on this responsibility.

It's a Cinch to Housebreak a Cat

Amazingly, cats seem automatically capable of using the litterbox from the moment you bring them home. Cats have a natural instinct to bury their waste—an instinct reinforced by watching their mothers perform the task. They love to be clean, and once they spot their litterbox, they will rarely eliminate outside of it (except in the case of some extenuating circumstance).

Cats Don't Need as Much Exercise as Dogs

Intense, regular exercise and play is a must for dogs. While a dog may chase you around begging to play ball all the time, cats don't need to be so active. Although they do need exercise and will chase a toy or grab at anything you dangle in front of them, you don't need to walk them or play with them constantly. In fact, if raised to stay indoors, cats are usually quite content doing so. They are generally rather quiet and usually not too rambunctious or destructive (with some exceptions).

Cats Require Less Training Than Dogs

Cats generally require less training than dogs, who must be taught rules and given restrictions in order to remain happy, well-behaved members of a family. For dogs, at least some level of obedience training is a must. Often, dog owners end up spending hundreds of dollars trying to solve their beloved canine's complicated behavioral problems. Most cats, however, behave well enough from the start, usually don't make messes, and basically mind their own business quite well.

CATS NEED LESS GROOMING THAN DOGS

Many dog breeds require a great deal of extra grooming. Even if you have a longhaired cat, grooming usually doesn't take as long as it would for a dog. In fact, shorthaired cats need very little, if any, grooming. Don't forget that cats usually keep themselves quite clean. Not so for a dog.

CATS ARE LESS AGGRESSIVE THAN DOGS

Landlords tend to be more tolerant of cat-owning tenants. No landlord wants to rent to a person who has an aggressive, dangerous dog. On the other hand, cats tend to show less aggression toward humans, and so they are not as much of a liability concern to landlords, who must now do business in a very litigious world.

CATS ARE MORE INDEPENDENT THAN DOGS

One reason why cats seem less removed from the wilder state of nature than dogs do is that they have not undergone the same intense level of domestication that dogs have. Because dogs are pack oriented, they learn intricate tasks quite well, which has allowed humans to use them in a wide variety of ways. Dogs adapt to new behaviors easily, and they have been genetically and behaviorally manipulated to suit particular tasks more than any other species of domestic animal. You need only look at two distinct dog breeds—take a Chihuahua or a Saint Bernard, for instance—to see the extreme range of canine diversity.

The bottom line is, because cats don't do the same variety of work that dogs do, their genes and their characters haven't been molded to the extreme, the way dogs' have been. Cats' ancient instincts have been preserved for the most part, leaving them with their characteristic "attitudes." Whether you find their particular attitudes annoying or amusing, you have to admire cats' independence and autonomy.

DOGS ARE MORE EMOTIONALLY NEEDY THAN CATS

Although some cats do constantly crave lots of love, hugs, and attention, for the most part, dogs are usually more demanding of your emotional energy. Lots of dogs beg for attention twenty-four seven, and this can get tough when you're tired, stressed out, or simply in need of some down time. You can't blame a pooch, though. Most dog breeds need tons of emotional input from their owners.

Cat Tales: The Best of Both Worlds

Having a cat will give you a unique combination taste of wild and domestic life. Cats are comfortable at home, yet still connected to their natural instincts. Sharing your life with a cat is like opening a secret window into the workings of nature. You can develop a respect for the prowess and athleticism of wild animals while still enjoying the companionship of a furry friend.

Cats, of course, don't bother with all the silly attention games. They like to be in charge of their own lives, and that's that. They come to you when they crave your companionship and then choose to walk away when they feel like amusing themselves. There are no manipulative head games and usually no ulterior motives—unless, of course, they are cozying up for food or some other type of treat! Otherwise, though, it is mostly just a matter of two equals interacting—at least in the cat's mind.

CATS ARE QUIETER THAN DOGS

Dogs bark. They have to; it's written into their job description. Dogs are more protective of the home than cats are, so dogs feel the need to warn their other pack members when potential invaders approach—

like the poor mail carrier or an unsuspecting neighbor. If you live in an apartment and have a noisy dog, you stand a good chance of being evicted. Most cats, on the other hand, are very quiet, and almost never raise their voices loud enough to make a fuss with the neighbors.

THE BOTTOM LINE

All of the above traits make cats easier to keep as pets than dogs, especially in a small apartment. Single people who work long hours are certainly more suited to having a cat instead of a dog. It's not only a matter of convenience, it's a matter of fairness to the dog. It's cruel to keep a dog in conditions that don't suit him. Why not get a cat, who seems custom-made for the position, instead?

Of course, cats do have certain tendencies that some people find hard to swallow. Cats are generally less overtly affectionate than dogs, and they certainly aren't as eager to please people. Being the parent of a freeloading feline can seem a thankless job—don't expect that cats will automatically show their appreciation for all the little things you do for them. Sometimes, these creatures seem to act as if it's your job to pamper them.

Cat Tales: Kitty Bonding

Because cats aren't instantly social with everyone they meet, some people assume they are coy, standoffish creatures. You might be surprised at how affectionate cats can really be. Many feline behaviorists comment on how cats sometimes seem to prefer human companionship to that of their own kind. Once they bond to their humans, cats think of us as parents or siblings rather than "owners."

While some felines are natural-born lap cats, others tire of being handled excessively, and they'll make a quick getaway, unlike dogs, who seem to thrive on touch. Because of this, don't automatically expect your cat to adore young children who overhandle animals or chase and tease them for long periods. A cat is not like a Golden Retriever, who will patiently tolerate poking, prodding, or tail pulling.

And, although cats can learn tricks, they usually won't learn them as quickly or perform them as consistently as dogs. Felines won't perform to please you; they need a major motivator—usually food—to entice them into action. And they have to be in a cooperative mood. Just don't expect your little feline fuzz ball to be catching Frisbees in her mouth any time soon!

Cat Tales: Kittenish Qualities

Most cats retain a certain kittenish quality throughout adulthood. For instance, they knead their humans with their paws. Kittens do this to stimulate milk production from their mother's teats. And they purr when we stroke them because kittens purr when nursing or when their mothers or siblings groom them.

Cats make excellent companions for those who can truly appreciate them. Cats are beautiful, graceful, compact, clean, sensitive, sleek, and beguiling. They possess a quiet, sinewy strength, a trait not seen in other pets. They are curious and can be very affectionate toward people they are familiar with—usually those who are smart enough to be gentle and patient, and know enough not to force their attentions upon cats. Once you do earn a cat's love and trust, she will brush against you, meow in your ear, gently paw your nose, curl up, and snuggle in your lap. And, as you lightly stroke her while she purrs contentedly, there is no more perfect state of bliss.

Adopting a Stray

So you've decided a cat is the right pet for you, and you're ready to run out to the nearest pet shop. Not so fast—first consider adopting a stray from a shelter. Cat overpopulation is a tremendous concern, and there is an overabundance of stray cats who need good homes. Before you do begin your search to adopt a stray, there are several things to keep in mind, including how to find a good animal shelter, which questions to ask, how to deal with health and behavioral issues, and more.

Most cats in this country and in the world are mixed-breed "rescue" cats obtained for little or no money from shelters. Pure-bred cats are in the numerical minority everywhere that cats are popular. This differs from the situation with purebred dogs, which constitute about one-third to one-half of all dogs in this country, and in the rest of the world. Unlike dogs, whose size and build differs greatly depending upon their breed, cat breeds are more similar, and there aren't nearly as many cat breeds as there are dog breeds. Consequently, adopting a mixed-breed cat is not all that different from having a pure-breed.

THE ETHICS OF ADOPTION

Every week in the United States, animal shelters euthanize thousands of cats because there are simply many more cats than there are potential families willing to give them homes. The number of purebred cats and kittens sold each year is a minute fraction of the number of the mixed-breed cats euthanized in the same time period; every purebred cat will easily find a home, and none are in jeopardy of losing their lives, simply due to their low supply and high demand. The euthanasia of homeless cats is a tragedy of epic proportions, caused by the ignorance and irresponsibility of current cat owners who neglect to have their pets spayed or neutered.

Cat Tales: Mixed-Breed Economics

A purebred kitty can run you anywhere from one hundred dollars for an unregistered cat to well over one or even two thousand dollars, depending on breed. On the other hand, a mixed-breed cat adopted from a shelter costs much less. Just be prepared to pay for neutering and vaccination costs. Many shelters will even give you a price break on initial veterinary services when you adopt a shelter cat, because they are so happy about your choice! A shelter will give you good kitty-parenting advice as well. Overall, a great deal, we'd say.

Shelter cats are no less intelligent than their purebred counterparts, they are just as healthy (if not more so), and they make equally fun and loving companions. The ethical question begs asking: In all good conscience, can you choose a purebred cat, knowing that so many mixed-breed cats are badly in need of homes?

National organizations such as the ASPCA and the Humane Society, in conjunction with local animal shelters, are working hard toward the goal of eliminating the unnecessary euthanasia of healthy, adoptable strays. There is good reason to hope this is an achievable goal within the next ten years. And, if every owner of a mixed-breed or pure-breed cat practices responsible ownership, the overpopulation problem will no longer exist. (For more on the no-kill shelter goal, visit the Best Friends Animal Society and Sanctuary Web site, at *www.bestfriends.org*.)

VARIETY IS THE SPICE OF MIXED-BREED LIFE

When you adopt a mixed-breed kitten, you don't really know, apart from her basic coat color, what you will end up with when she grows. Will she have long legs and a skinny body, or short legs and a stocky, powerful build? You'll just have to wait and see. While some people prefer the pre-dictability of breed standards, this sort of variety can be quite fun—and it's a sure shot that your little mixed-breed kitten will be a unique, one-of-a-kind masterpiece unlike any other when she grows up!

Temperament is also a tossup when it comes to mixed breeds. You just can't predict what that little shelter kitten's personality is going to be like, unless you observe at least one of his parents (often an impossibility) or his siblings.

Although you might not know exactly what kind of personality you'll end up with, don't fret too much about this. If you carefully observe a kitten at play or interact with him before you adopt him, you'll get some idea of his personality. Don't forget, a lot depends on the way you raise your kitty. (Remember the good old nature-versus-nurture debate? The combination applies here, too.) Chances are, if you are a mindful and attentive kitty parent, you will be able to make the most of your kitten's personality strengths while also gently cor-recting his less-than-ideal tendencies.

Healthy Stock

Because mixed breeds (whose purebred ancestors are at least three or four generations removed) have drawn their genes from a much larger gene pool than have purebred cats, they may be some-what less prone to developing anatomical, physiological, or behavioral abnormalities. Mixed-breed cats generally have fewer musculoskeletal problems and stronger immune systems than do purebred cats. First-generation mixed-breed cats from purebred parents, though, have little or no advantage over purebred cats.

CHOOSING YOUR SHELTER CAT

If you choose to rescue a mixed-breed cat from a shelter, bravo! You are doing a wonderful thing, you know. The first place to check is your local SPCA or Humane Society. Also check smaller local animal shelters, or any other town-run shelters in your area. Though not necessarily as well funded as the county or the Humane Society shelters, most of these do an admirable job caring for their "rescue" animals with the money derived primarily through donations and fees charged for animal adoptions.

Cat Tales: Purebred Shelter Cats

Don't assume that shelters have only mixed-breed cats and kittens available for adoption. Every now and then a nice American shorthair, Siamese, Persian, or other purebred feline shows up. Usually these adult cats have been abandoned or lost, and they need your help as much as the mixed breeds.

Most shelters run a considerate, efficient ship, and they normally have informed, polite staff members who can help you choose a kitty and answer questions you may have regarding procedures, supplies, proper environment for the cat, healthy diet, and where to find a good vet. Typically, these places also offer some sort of pet counseling as well as workshops on proper pet parenting.

Both private and public shelters usually provide low-cost neutering services (usually a mandatory condition of adoption). The neutering fee is included in the overall adoption fee. Many shelters will also provide you with some food and litter, and perhaps even a litterbox and a toy or two.

Above all, if possible, never take home a kitten who is under eight weeks old. Kittens who have left their mothers and litters too soon may show profound fear, aggression, and antisocial behavior toward others. If you do unexpectedly become the parent of an extremely young kitten (this can occur sometimes, when kittens are unfortunately separated from their mothers), you will have to work extra hard to raise a healthy, secure, and well-adjusted kitty.

Clean Bill of Health

While handling kittens at a shelter, examine them closely and observe their general health. A kitten's coat should be clean and relatively unmatted; there should be no missing patches or scabbing, which could point to parasitic infections or allergies. The kitten's eyes, ears, and nose should be free of discharge. Watch for bloated bellies—usually a sign of worms. Be sure the kitten's ribs aren't sticking out. Also check for any skeletal problems such as malformed legs, paws, spine, or jaw. Even check the kitten's teeth and gums. An eight-week-old should have a full set of milk teeth, and her gums should be pink.

Stay away from any kitten who is sneezing, scratching incessantly, or seems dull, listless, or scrawny. Look for any signs of diarrhea in the animals' enclosure (also for dried feces around the anal area). Observe whether or not kittens are using their litterbox. Choosing one who already has this skill down pat will save you a lot of aggravation at home!

Smart Shelter Questions

Learn as much as you can about a cat or kitten before adopting one from the shelter. Here are some key questions to ask:

- Why is the cat or kitten up for adoption?

- Who were the previous owners?

- Was the animal abused, as far as you know?

- Are the kitten's littermates present? (If so, ask to see them all together.)

- Is their mother there also? (Ask to see her as well.)

- Can I spend more than a few minutes with the cat or kitten before making a decision?

- Has a veterinarian examined the cat and checked for potentially serious illnesses?

- Has the cat or kitten been fully vaccinated?

- Has the animal shown any kind of antisocial or aggressive behavior?

Big or Small?

Pay attention to size (relative to age). Does one kitten seem stockier and larger-boned than the others? Does another seem long-legged and thin? Determining what size a mixed-breed kitten will ultimately be is not totally impossible; if you are looking for a particular build of cat, it won't hurt to try to determine this at an early stage.

Social Butterflies

Shelters normally keep kittens together; this will allow you to evaluate their sociability and determine which ones are dominant, submissive, curious, timid, or confident. Consider a kitten only after you've seen him interacting with other kittens. Look for a kitten who seems at ease around others and shows a relaxed yet inquisitive nature toward you. Ball up a sheet of paper and toss it in among the kittens; see who gets to it first, and what the general reaction of the group is. A kitten who wants to play and shows no concern is probably a good choice. Avoid selecting any kitten who seems fearful of you or the other kittens; this type could exhibit antisocial behavior problems later on. Avoid any kitten who swats or hisses at you or the other kittens in unprovoked anger or fear.

FINDING KITTIES IN THE CLASSIFIEDS

The abundance of mixed-breed kittens listed in the Classifieds is proof positive that many owners are still irresponsible about spaying and neutering their pets. Although it's an unfortunate problem, this irresponsibility may inadvertently lead you to the right kitten. First, if you go to a private home to adopt a kitten, you will get to see the mother and perhaps the entire litter. It's a great advantage if you can see the mother's temperament. If she is extremely timid and antisocial, think twice about adopting one of her kittens, who could easily have inherited her undesirable personality. If the mother seems confident, curious, and at ease in your presence, chances are her kittens will behave similarly later in life.

Visit kittens who are in the seven- to eight-week-old range; by this time their mother will be attempting to distance herself physically and emotionally from her kittens, who in the wild are self-sufficient by the fourth month. Seeing an entire litter of kittens will give you the chance to compare and contrast them behaviorally, allowing you to choose the one who seems most at ease with you. Be sure to observe and test each available kitten using the methods discussed in the preceding section. Kittens from the same litter have been with each other from birth and are more at ease with themselves and their environment. You can get a better feel for each cat's true temperament.

Even if you adopt a kitten from a private owner, you'll still need to pick up the tab for spaying or neutering, vaccinations, and other health concerns.

Cat Tales: Home Sweet Home?

Going to the home where the kittens were born allows you to see firsthand just what type of conditions they were raised under. If the place is a pigsty and the owners have twelve pregnant females roaming the property, it's time to shove off. If the place is clean and the owners are easygoing and kind to you and the animals, you can probably assume that the kittens are well cared for and relatively healthy.

STRAY CATS

How many of us have unsuspectingly opened our front doors, only to encounter a scruffy kitty meowing at us? After feeding and petting the poor little foundling for a few days, all but the most disciplined weaken; most of us will soon take the cat into our homes, set up an appointment with the veterinarian, name the waif, and make her a part of our family.

Strays often make great pets; they seem to be very appreciative and particularly loyal to the person who saved them. There are, however, some health issues to consider if you've adopted a stray. Be careful if you have other pets in your home, because many of these problems can be passed on from animal to animal via saliva through sharing food, biting, or even mutual grooming. Have your stray examined and, if necessary, treated for the following problems:

- Feline leukemia, feline immunodeficiency virus, and feline infectious peritonitis, all deadly viral contagions.

- Internal and external parasites, including various types of worms, fleas, and ticks.

- Injuries received during fights with other strays or with dogs, including cuts, abscesses from bites, and broken or sprained limbs.

- Ear infections, intestinal disorders, or eye problems.

Remember, since strays have not usually been vaccinated against anything, there's a chance they could be carrying the rabies virus, which is deadly to all mammals, including humans. Once your stray is examined and it's determined that she doesn't have rabies, be sure to have her vaccinated properly!

Behavioral Concerns

Most strays who have been out on the street for a while have endured a lot of heartache. Owners have abandoned or abused them. Animals have attacked them. Cars have tried to run them over. Consequently, they tend to be shy, skittish, and much less sociable initially. Some might also show aggression toward other pets, at least at first. Because life on the streets has probably taught them some hard lessons, they are often less trusting, and they develop a certain timidity out of the need to survive. Strays may not be as open to being touched or held as would a cat you have raised yourself; they may try to scratch or bite those who get too chummy too fast. A family with children should, therefore, be especially careful when adopting a stray.

Cat Tales: Teaching an Older Cat New Tricks

Often, it's not as easy to teach an older cat as it is a kitten. In fact, any adult cat, be it a stray or not, has well-established behavior that will be more difficult to modify. Be prepared to put a lot of effort into training an adult cat.

Many strays will still whine to go outside. Be cautious about letting your cat outside. Remember, if you accede to his cries of "*let me out*," he'll run the risk of getting into catfights, and he might pick up viruses and parasites and bring them home to your other pets.

Some strays also refuse to use a litterbox for a while, due to inexperience or lack of practice, or from having to exert dominance over other strays by leaving feces unburied. It may take some time, but they will eventually get it. Just be patient—with some direction and much-needed love and attention, your stray should make great strides.

If you do encounter a stray but decide you don't have the ability to care for him, bring him to the nearest shelter or find him a good home by other means, so that he will have the chance to be adopted by a willing, patient person.

The Long and Short of It

Mixed-breed cats are more frequently shorthaired, but there are longhaired mixed breeds as well. Both varieties shed; you'll just have more to vacuum up with a longhaired cat. Longhaired cats require more grooming, whereas shorthaired felines don't need as much brushing or overall coat care. Shorthaired cats also have less of a problem with hairballs. If you decide on a longhaired cat, be prepared to brush and comb him on a weekly basis to reduce shedding and keep the coat mat-free and healthy.

On average, longhaired cats tend to be slightly less active and more reserved than shorthaired cats. If you want a more active cat and hate brushing and vacuuming, a shorthaired cat might be right for you. If you don't mind brushing and prefer a more laid-back pet, a longhaired cat will be great.

ROOM FOR ONE MORE?

Though cats are okay being on their own and can amuse themselves quite well throughout the day, it might be a good idea to consider adopting two kittens instead of one, particularly if you live alone and are gone for a good part of the day. Cats who spend most of the day alone tend to get into things they shouldn't. A bored or nervous cat may destroy houseplants, rip apart sofas, become overly vocal, or even forget her litterbox etiquette. Being alone too long can be stressful, even for a cat; this stress can eventually result in poor health.

Here are some advantages to adopting two littermates:

1. They will amuse each other, preventing property destruction and separation anxiety.

2. They will learn to be more sociable than kittens raised alone. This may make bringing future animals into the home easier.

3. They will retain a vestige of kittenhood into adulthood, making them more playful and accepting of strangers.

Two mixed-breed kittens won't cost much more than one. Sure, there's the additional spaying or neutering costs, and you'll have to buck up for double the vaccinations. But if you're going to go out and invest in a litterbox, scratching post, cat toys, and such anyway, why not have two cats? Best of all, you will be saving two lives instead of just one.

In general, however, it's not a good idea to adopt more than two at a time; the social dynamics change with three or more cats. Territorial problems are more likely to crop up, leading to fighting and injury. So you should consider waiting a while before adopting other cats.

AGE HAS ITS BENEFITS

Adopting an adult or adolescent cat can have advantages; read on.

1. An older cat is more likely to act the way a well-behaved cat should. She'll probably be much less destructive around the house.

2. An adult cat's personality is already formed, so you know what you're dealing with.

3. An adult cat is more likely to be trained to use a litterbox.

4. An older cat is precisely the size it is going to be, so there are no surprises.

There are disadvantages to adopting an adult cat, as well.

1. An adult cat's behavior patterns can be harder to modify. If some of the cat's behaviors are undesirable, it could spell trouble.

2. An adult cat in a shelter is going to be much more stressed than a kitten, because he will not be happy about being around so many other cats and dogs.

3. An adult cat in a shelter was either lost, wild, or abandoned; this means he had a life he was accustomed to but now misses. Cats are creatures of habit, and when suddenly removed from what they are used to, they become stressed and worried.

Because of these last two stress-creating problems, it may be hard for you to accurately determine what an adult shelter cat's true personality is like. Adopting one out of a private home is probably a better idea; you can get a better feel for its temperament when it is still in its relaxed home environment.

Unless they are littermates or have been together since a young age, adopting more than one adult cat from two different places is not a great idea. If you do go this route, be forewarned that they will probably be very territorial with each other, and you might have to referee plenty of battles.

Finding a Purebred

If your heart is set on having a purebred, you'll have to choose from the forty or so cat breeds currently recognized by the numerous national and international cat associations in existence today. Above all, never get a cat from a pet store—these cruel, kitty-mill businesses should be avoided at all costs. You need some smart guidelines for finding a good breeder, and once you do, you need to know what questions to ask.

A purebred cat could cost you a pretty penny and then some. Breeders are in business, after all, and must make a profit to remain successful. You also pay for the uniqueness of the breed; purebred cats are far less common than mixed breeds, and certain breeds are down-right hard to find. You always pay more for that which is in demand.

PREDICTABLE PATTERNS

Unlike mixed-breed cats, with a purebred kitten, what you see is pretty much what you will get. A pure-breed's genes have been closely crafted, and this will control the cat's appearance. A Havana brown in Arkansas, for example, is going to look just like a Havana brown in Peru. You'll know exactly what your kitty will look like fully grown even before she grows up.

Purebred cats' temperaments are also quite predictable, owing once again to the control exerted over each breed's genes. All Persians will be somewhat reserved, just as all Siamese will be lively and vocal. Those things are pretty much givens.

Although purebred cats can be more likely to inherit health problems, most breeders do an admirable job of weeding out undesirable traits from their stock. The problem isn't as serious as you might think, as long as you deal with a reputable breeder.

Cat Tales: Breeding Opportunities

Breeding cats should not be taken lightly, and it's not something you do to make a fast buck—it's usually not very profitable. Most breeders do it out of love for their particular breed, barely covering their costs. Do not breed cats if your only motivation is to show your kids "the miracle of birth." If you really want them to learn something, take them to a shelter to see all the unwanted kittens.

If you're trying to determine which breed is right for you, look at cat magazines and attend cat shows to better acquaint yourself with the breeds that interest you.

GOOD BREEDING

Once you decide on the right breed, locate a reputable breeder. All reputable breeders should:

1. Have their purebred cats properly registered with a reputable cat association such as the CFA (Cat Fanciers Association). The CFA will determine whether pedigree information is accurate, and will also (for a fee) add your kitty's name to its pedigree and send you a registration certificate. If a breeder has not properly registered his or her cats and will not provide you with a pedigree, walk on.

2. Strictly abide by the breed "standard"—the physical characteristics that set a breed apart from all others. Familiarize yourself with the standards of your favorite breeds; if a breeder's cats do not match closely, move on. Careless or greedy breeders will sell kittens or cats who are bad representatives of the breed.

3. Allow you to examine their cats for any basic structural flaws, including:

- Kinked tail
- Severe underbite or overbite
- Polydactyly (too many toes on a foot)
- Pronounced limp, indicating hip, shoulder, spine, or leg problems
- Improper coat color or length
- Incorrect head shape
- Incorrect tail length
- Improper build
- Incorrect eye color

4. Be as curious about you as you are about their cats. Dedicated breeders want their kittens to go to people who love and care for them properly. If a breeder puts you through the wringer, be thankful; he or she is a concerned professional who is looking for more than just a buyer. If a breeder wants to know nothing about you apart from the color of your money, this is a bad sign.

5. Take great care in deciding which two cats to breed, rather than just putting any female in heat together with a willing male. Bad breeders will mate any two cats to make a buck.

6. Keep cats in a top-notch, clean cattery. Any breeders who allow their cats' environment to become filthy or overcrowded show a lack of concern and professionalism, and should be avoided.

7. Socialize kittens with other cats and people from a very early age, and also handle the kittens from the first week on, to ensure that they will be happy and confident with people. Avoid any breeder who isolates kittens from human contact or claims early socialization is bad.

8. Attend and compete in cat shows on a regular basis, to keep their skills on a competitive level and to remain in touch with trends. Stay away from a breeder who shuns cat shows.

Finding a Breeder

So, where do you find these wonderful, caring, altruistic cat breeders? There are a number of options, including the following.

- **Clubs:** Most cat breeds have a club dedicated to the betterment and discussion of that breed. Locate these breed clubs by contacting one of the well-known cat registries listed in the Appendix. Any breed club should be more than happy to provide you with information on their breed and to give you a list of reputable breeders in your area.

- **Magazines:** Newsstand publications such as *Cat Fancy* and *Cats* magazine always contain breeder advertising. Reading these may help you to locate a reputable local breeder.

- **Veterinarians:** Your local vet knows a healthy cat when she sees one. Ask her to recommend a good breeder in your area or put you in contact with a client who owns an outstanding representative of the breed you like. That owner could help you to connect with the cat's breeder.

- **Cat shows:** Good breeders attend and compete at local and national cat shows. Attend some and talk to the breeders present. Get a feel for their competence while observing their cats firsthand. See who wins, and get that breeder's card!

- **Classified ads:** Good breeders and lousy ones alike advertise in the classifieds, so contact and visit a number of breeders before making any decisions.

Once you have identified several breeders of good reputation, make an appointment to visit their catteries and follow the guidelines explained earlier in this chapter. Look for cleanliness and professionalism. Observe the adult cats, and pay attention to your gut instincts regarding the breeder.

When you have finally chosen a breeder, it might take a while before he or she has kittens available. Use the same selection criteria set forth in Chapter 3 for choosing your cat.

Other Considerations

There are additional concerns when selecting a purebred kitten. Price will vary according to whether the kitten is "show" quality or "pet" quality. All this means is that a kitten with features considered "perfect" for the breed has potential to be a cat-show champion, and will therefore be more expensive. On the other hand, a kitten with a slight flaw, such as the wrong color coat or too short a face, will cost appreciably less, yet still be just as healthy and well adjusted.

Expect that a breeder will want to find people who will properly care for kittens, raise them in a suitable environment, and abide by the breeder's contractual stipulations. These could include clauses requiring neutering, indoor-only living, and prohibition of declawing.

Cat Tales: Show Cat versus Family Pet

Most breeders have both "show" quality and "pet" quality kittens. Show-quality kittens could eventually be entered into competition, and might possibly do quite well. Although the pet-quality kittens have some minor flaw in structure or appearance that would prevent them from doing well at a show, they will still make great pets. If you don't care about showing or breeding your cat, you should seriously consider purchasing a pet-quality cat, provided the "flaw" is not severe or debilitating.

BREEDER Q & A

Once you locate a breeder with whom you feel comfortable, you will need to ask some important questions, including the following.

1. When will you have kittens available? Good breeders do not have kittens available year-round; only "kitten mills" and profit-motivated breeding facilities do. If you are dedicated to purchasing a purebred, you may have to wait until one is available.

2. At what age will you let your kittens go home with their new owners? No breeder worth his salt will let a kitten go before she is at least ten weeks old. Remember, kittens who leave their mothers and litters too soon do not become properly socialized and may grow into antisocial adults. Also, kittens under ten weeks of age will not have been fully vaccinated or wormed.

3. Are your kittens raised in the home or in cages? Most good breeders raise their kittens indoors, so they can become accustomed to the goings-on of a normal home. Kittens raised in cages in the garage will not be nearly as friendly or well adjusted.

4. How many breeding adult cats do you have? Beware of any breeder who has more than eight or ten breeding cats on the premises. Any more than that and it smacks of a kitten-mill operation. Dedicated breeders don't care about the number of kittens produced, only their quality.

5. Do you currently own any breeding Champions or Grand Champions? All breeders strive to have one or more of their breeding cats win a cat show. You can be sure that kittens who come from prize-winning stock will be great examples of their breed. Poor breeders who are interested only in high volume and profit don't have adequate breeding stock on hand to win cat shows.

6. Are your cats regularly tested for feline leukemia? This fatal infectious disease can wipe out an entire cattery and spread throughout the entire locale. A good breeder will have a veterinarian regularly test for this killer.

7. What type of guarantees do you give on your kittens? Any good breeder will provide a buyer with a two- or three-week guarantee for the kitten's general health, and a six-month guarantee against congenital defects. If a breeder will not agree to these terms, pass on her kittens.

8. Do you fully vaccinate and worm the kittens? All good breeders see to this. If the breeder says it is your responsibility, go elsewhere.

9. What is included in your contract? A responsible breeder should provide a buyer with a comprehensive contract that includes the following:

- A written health guarantee, including a warranty against congenital defects
- The kitten's date of birth and description
- A written bill of sale including the price paid and date of purchase
- Registration papers, including the kitten's registration number
- The kitten's pedigree
- Any conditional clauses, including those covering neutering, declawing, and indoor living only
- Instructions on diet, worming, vaccinations, and general care
- A record of vaccinations and wormings to date
- A photo of the kitten

10. Will you provide a veterinary health certificate? All responsible breeders should offer these.

11. Will you provide references? Dedicated breeders will gladly offer a list of happy customers. If they hedge on this, it compromises their credibility.

12. May I inspect your cattery? Good breeders have nothing to hide. As long as you do not disturb nursing mothers, this shouldn't be a problem. A poor breeder may balk at this request because of terrible, crowded, or dirty conditions in the cattery.

13. Should I leave a deposit? In order to ensure that the kitten of your choice is still available when the time does come to take her home, the breeder may ask you for a deposit. Be suspicious of any breeder who asks for more than one hundred dollars, unless the breed is extremely rare.

14. Will you accept a check or a credit card in lieu of cash? Be wary of a breeder who does a cash-only business, as this is often the hallmark of a fly-by-night operation. Paying by check or credit card allows you to void the transaction the next day if foul play or fraud should be detected.

Cat Tales: Boy or Girl?

Deciding on whether you want a male or female cat or kitten should not be a big issue. Overall, males and females behave quite similarly, with just a few differences. Males tend to be slightly more outgoing and curious, whereas females might be more reserved. Males are usually slightly larger on average, they tend to roam more, and could be more combative. But some females can really go at it, too. These are just broad guidelines, however; remember, individual behavior varies tremendously from cat to cat.

A Warning about Pet Shops

Never ever buy your kitten from a pet shop. Pet shops get their kittens from "kitty mills," large breeding facilities that pump out thousands of poor-quality kittens each year. These animals are made to live in atrocious conditions, they are usually structurally and behaviorally unsound, and they often have diseases or infections. They get to interact with their mothers or littermates for no more than a week or two before they are shipped off, so they are usually antisocial and very stressed out. Resist the urge to buy the first cute kitten you see in a store window on impulse—don't support this cruel, breed-destroying business. *Avoid pet shops at all costs!*

Bringing Your Kitty Home

K itties are mischievous, curious little creatures who get into anything and everything. Before you bring yours home, kitty-proofing your house is a must! Also be prepared in advance with basic supplies, such as food and water dishes, a litterbox, a scratching post, a travel crate, toys, grooming supplies, a collar and identification tag, and a first-aid kit. From introducing your cat to your children and other pets, to showing your cat the lay of the land and setting up a routine, this chapter will teach you what you need to know to help your cat get acclimated to her new home.

TIME TO SETTLE IN

Once your fur ball comes barreling into your home, the first thing you need to do is set aside some time for quality bonding together. Before you rush back to work and leave the little cutie pie all alone for the day, get acquainted and make your new pet feel at ease. Remember, your kitty is in unfamiliar territory; it will take time for her to get used to her new surroundings.

The best possible scenario is bringing the cat home at the beginning of a vacation. Not only will a week or two together help you to bond, it will also give you a chance to work out any kinks in your system. You'll learn about your cat's unique personality, and your cat will also begin to learn the "do's and don'ts" of living with you. If a full week isn't possible, at least shoot to bring your cat home on a three-day weekend.

INSIDE OR OUT?

Decide whether or not your cat will have access to the outdoors *before* bringing him home. Today, most neighborhoods, particularly urban ones, are rife with feline dangers, diseases, and death. Your cat could be bitten, infected, or killed by a dog, raccoon, or another cat defending its territory. Likewise, countless numbers of cats get killed each year because of traffic and other unfortunate side effects caused by the hectic, crazed environment we humans have engineered.

Outdoor cats live significantly shorter lives than their indoor counterparts. They suffer more injuries, become less sociable with people and other animals, and land themselves in the veterinarian's office more often than they should. The simplest way to increase your cat's lifespan significantly is by keeping him inside your home.

Keeping your cat indoors will also prevent him from preying on small wild creatures such as songbirds who wouldn't naturally have hordes of domestic cats running around trying to kill them. These poor little creatures have a hard enough time on their own without our pets upsetting the natural balance of things.

Cat Tales: Consistency Is Key

Cats, like kids, require consistency. They need a predictable, safe environment free from hidden surprises or unexpected trauma. Set up a scheduled routine for your cat by feeding, grooming, and playing with him at the same time each day, and in the same place. Try to wake up and go to sleep at fairly predictable times. And, most important, stick to whatever rules you have set down for your cat!

As long as you provide your cat with a stimulating home environment, he won't have any need to go outdoors. Cats kept inside from kittenhood on usually don't miss going outside, because the home is their territory, and they don't feel any need to leave it.

An adopted older cat might at first insist on going outside if that's what she's been used to. She will probably sit by a window and cry, and she'll try to scoot out of open doors, too. Be aware of that, and inform family and friends to be careful, too. After four or five months, she'll most likely accept the new situation and claim the home as her new territory.

Some people say it's cruel to deny an animal access to the outdoors, but it's crueler to cater to a cat's desires when you know it could cause her harm. The real cruelty lies in allowing your cat to roam around unsupervised. If you really feel you want your cat to have some fresh air or experience the outdoors, either train her to walk on a leash, or allow her to go outside only in a small, safe area from which she won't escape, such as an enclosed balcony or a roofed play area you build in the back yard. And never leave her outside unsupervised!

KITTY-PROOFING YOUR HOME

Make your home environment safe *before* kitty moves in. Cats (especially kittens) have a knack for getting into every nook and cranny of your home, including the tops of appliances and cabinets. They even find ways to squeeze into or under pieces of furniture that no dog could ever dream of getting at. Here are some suggestions for safeguarding your feline's new environment:

1. Check all possible escape routes, making sure that your cat has no way of accessing the outdoors. If a new cat gets outside within the first few days, he won't yet have a clear sense of where "home" is. He could be killed or taken by another cat lover.

2. Install childproof locks on the cupboards and drawers, even on ones that contain no dangerous materials. You don't want your cat to learn how to open these or get into something potentially toxic. You also don't want to come home to find the pantry torn apart!

3. Put baby guard plugs on all unused electric sockets. A curious little paw could poke around enough to get a fatal surprise.

4. Minimize power cords and wires. Kittens will play with and possibly gnaw on them, and in doing so may be shocked or killed. Put wires under carpets when possible, or tack them securely along moldings or under furniture. Out of sight, out of mind.

5. Remove all potentially toxic chemicals from your cat's domain. Everyone has household cleaners, bleach, insecticides, drain cleaners, or solvents under their kitchen sinks; make sure you attach a secure baby guard to this cupboard to prevent your cat from ingesting poison. Do not assume that something stored high up is out of the cat's reach. You have to think in three dimensions with a cat. New cat owners, particularly those used to having only dogs, can be especially vulnerable to this mistake. Remember, cats can jump and climb like crazy!

Poisonous Plants

Cats like to chew on houseplants, so you should be aware from the start that many ordinary house and garden plants can be toxic, even in small amounts. The following is a list of toxic plants:

- Azalea
- Bean plants
- Cactus
- Crocus
- Daffodil
- Dieffenbachia
- Hemlock
- Hydrangea
- Ivy
- Lily
- Marijuana
- Mistletoe

- Mushroom
- Narcissus
- Nightshade
- Oleander
- Philodendron
- Poinsettia
- Potato leaves
- Rhododendron
- Tobacco
- Tomato leaves
- Walnut
- Yew

If your cat ever ingests any of these plants, call your vet immediately. (For more information, refer to the ASPCA's Poison Control Center, at *www.aspca.org*.)

STOCKING UP ON SUPPLIES

Every new pet needs a few essentials. Make sure you have the following items ready when kitty comes home.

Chow Time

Nutritious food is essential. If you're unsure about what to feed your cat, talk to your breeder, shelter, or veterinarian to get an educated suggestion. Kittens need different food from adult cats; they require higher amounts of protein, fat, vitamins, and minerals. Always have a good dry food on hand, and consider supplementing it with canned food. Foods available at a pet shop will be of higher quality than supermarket-brand foods. Diet will be discussed in more detail later in this book.

Food and Water Dishes

Nothing fancy needed here; a four- to six-inch-diameter hard plastic or metal bowl for food and the same for water will do just fine. Some owners opt for an "extended feeder" type apparatus that meters either food or water down into a dish as the cat needs it. Available in most pet supply stores, this comes in handy if you go away on vacation for a few days and can't find anyone to come in to feed your cat.

Cat Tales: Avoid Hazardous Toys

Never give your cat toys that have small plastic pieces, buttons, rivets, or beads; they could chew them off and choke. Or, if swallowed, these things can cause intestinal blockages. Also avoid giving your cat home-made toys that could be toxic or harmful to his digestive tract, such as empty plastic jars or bottles that once contained chemicals or medications, balls of aluminum foil (if swallowed, foil can cause perforations or blockages), ribbons, or rubber bands.

Place your cat's dishes in a spot that is easy to clean and where there will be as few interruptions as possible. Cats can be finicky eaters; placing the food dish in a highly trafficked spot may prevent them from eating properly. A quiet corner in the kitchen is fine, provided you are not cooking some masterful meal that has you flying around the room and smells really tempting.

Process of Elimination

Cats are tidy little devils who prefer to bury their waste. Fortunately, humans can capitalize on this instinct. Your cat's litterbox should be made of a durable plastic so that it can be easily cleaned and will not absorb and retain odors. Clumping and crystal litters are the most convenient. The first allows you to scoop out clumps; the second lets you scoop solid waste but it also absorbs urine quite well.

If you are bringing home a kitten, consider purchasing a box that is only two to three inches high, so the little one can have easy access. Older cats will do better with a box that is four inches high or more, to prevent them from scattering litter all over the room. Covered litterboxes allow the cat some additional privacy, which is useful when there is more than one cat in the household. Most covered litterboxes have a removable top; keep the top off at first, until the cat begins using the box on a regular basis. If you do have more than one cat, it might be a good idea to get them separate litterboxes. This will help prevent arguments and the accidents that can follow.

Scratch up a Storm!

Cats scratch to shed worn claw coverings and to help them visually mark their territories. Your cat will want to scratch something on a daily basis. To prevent your sofa from becoming the object of your cat's scratching passion, get him a nice, tall scratching post, one that is at least three feet high, four to six inches in diameter, and covered with carpet, rope, or some other textured, interesting material. Some people even go whole hog, either purchasing or building a four- to six-foot-high "kitty condo" structure—a multileveled, carpet-covered playland that most cats love. If you have room for one in your home, it's great to have. Kitty playlands provide cats with lots of stimulation, preventing boredom and consequent destructive behavior.

One good way to train your cat to scratch on his post is to place it near where your cat sleeps or naps; cats prefer scratching right after waking up, much like the way we humans like to stretch.

Cat Tales: The Pains of Teething

Between the ages of three and six months, your kitten's permanent teeth will come in, and he may be uncomfortable—as evidenced by his random meowing and incessant chewing on whatever he can get his mouth on. Make sure that you have a few tough rubber or hard plastic toys around for him to chew on. Your vet can also give you a topical ointment that, when applied to the kitten's gums, will relieve pain. Don't use ointments designed for humans—they could be toxic to a kitten.

Sleepy Time

Many of you will want your cat to sleep with you, and that's fine—your adorable little feline will probably con you into it one way or another. For those of you who have wills strong enough to resist the wiles of a purring, cuddly feline eager to snuggle with you, go ahead and invest in a cat bed. It should be comfy and warm enough to make your cat want to curl up on it. Get something that has a washable cover and is large enough for the cat to stretch out on. Don't spend too much, though. Cats are finicky; they prefer to choose their beds themselves—and they usually choose yours. You're likely to find them curled up in a comfy chair, or else in some other more ridiculous space, like a basket, box, open suitcase, or anywhere else that's not the bed you bought for them. You don't want to get stuck with an empty cat bed that cost you fifty bucks.

Play Time

Your cat needs plenty of stimulation to keep her busy and out of trouble in her new home while you're gone. Playing *with* your cat will also be important and fun; it's a way to bond, and it also helps your young feline friend to develop coordination.

Give your cat a variety of teaser toys, fake mice, windup toys, small rubber balls, or crocheted balls with catnip inside. But you don't necessarily have to spend a lot of money to entertain your little bugger. Try giving your cat a cardboard box or paper grocery bag; she will love to play hide and seek, and she'll go nuts for the crunchy sound of the paper.

On the Road

A plastic travel crate is a safe way to transport your cat in a car. Have your travel crate with you when you pick up your cat for the first time. Most cats don't enjoy car rides because of all the hectic, uncontrollable activity going on around them. Often, being loose in a car is like being in a fishbowl; the cat feels vulnerable, restrained, and powerless. Putting your cat in a travel crate for trips to the vet or to the cat sitter will make him feel safe, keep him more relaxed, and help him to feel in control.

Most pet shops sell good-quality, airline-approved travel crates; make sure the crate is large enough for a full-grown cat, but small enough to fit beneath the seat of an airplane. Keep a comfy pad or blanket in it for warmth and security. When traveling by car, always place the crate in a safe, secure area. The floor or back seat of the car is best.

As your cat becomes accustomed to riding in cars, you can eventually hold her in your lap while someone else drives, but because that first car ride can be quite nerve-wracking, you don't want to risk her getting loose and interfering with the driving in some way.

ID Collar

Even if you keep your cat indoors all the time, it's still possible for a door or window to be left open accidentally, providing your feline explorer with an avenue to the outside world. Make sure he wears a collar with a clearly legible identification tag on it at all times. Consider an elastic or "breakaway" collar; either will prevent your cat from choking should the collar snag on something.

Introduce the collar to your cat early, so you don't encounter resistance. If your cat doesn't take to wearing a collar, try putting the collar on for a minute at a time, and offer your cat's favorite treat or toy during that brief period, to keep her attention off the collar. Repeat the exercise daily, slowly lengthening the duration of time the collar is worn.

THE WELL-GROOMED CAT

Grooming is important, especially for longhaired felines. Apart from keeping your cat looking good, grooming her from an early age will also help her to grow accustomed to being handled regularly. This will come in especially handy when you need to check her for parasites or injury.

Most pet shops carry a wide assortment of grooming tools, so you should be able to find what you need easily.

Brush

Regular brushing helps to remove loose, dead hairs from the cat's coat and reduce the occurrence of hairballs. Not to mention it helps to keep your home hair-free. Choose a soft, slicker-type brush for your shorthaired cat; it will get the job done and not feel harsh on the cat's skin. For a longhaired cat, use a brush more like one a human might use.

Comb

Longhaired felines need to be combed after being brushed. Combing removes mats and tangles, which, when not untangled, can be irritating to the cat's skin. And you certainly don't want to cut stubborn snarls out of your cat's coat! Use a wide comb first, then follow up with a finer-toothed comb.

Nail Clippers

Cats with untrimmed nails can wreak havoc on furniture, rugs, wallpaper, and anything else they can dig their sharp little claws into. Start trimming your cat's nails during kittenhood, so that he will learn to tolerate it fairly well. Pet supply stores do sell special kitty nail clippers, but "human" nail clippers work just as well.

Bubble Up

You shouldn't have to bathe your cat often; they're clean little devils. Nevertheless, the day will come where your little devil will get herself into a particularly dirty or oily mess, so make sure you have good cat shampoo and conditioner on hand. Don't use products made for humans—they will irritate kitty's skin. Check out the good old local pet shop for better options.

FELINE FIRST-AID KIT

Though you should always take your cat to the vet immediately for any ailment you suspect might be serious, be prepared to deal with minor problems, such as colds, small cuts, bruises, abrasions, tick removal, and so on. And, if your cat ever becomes seriously injured or ill, you might be able to save her life if a veterinarian is not available right away. (See Chapters 10 and 11 for more in-depth first-aid techniques.)

Your feline first-aid kid should include:

- A rectal thermometer

- A small penlight

- Tweezers

- Hydrogen Peroxide

- Rubbing alcohol

- Disinfecting solution

- An antibacterial scrub

- A small blanket

- Gauze pads and a roll of gauze

- Adhesive tape

- Cotton swabs

- Mineral oil

- A stethoscope

You should be able to find all of these things in your local pharmacy.

THE LAY OF THE LAND

When setting up for the arrival of your new friend, the best thing you can do is to make your home environment pleasant, calm, and quiet, so your cat can feel at ease from the start. Cats are creatures of routine, and they want to be in a predictable, safe environment. Kitty won't be too pleased if he's thrown into a hectic home filled with intrusive, frightening disturbances.

Show your cat where all the necessities are right away. Make sure you've already put out some food and water (place those dishes in a low-traffic area). It's equally important to show the cat where his litterbox is located. Set your cat down right in the box, then scratch your fingers in the fresh litter a few times. Even a ten-week-old kitten will catch on quickly. Make sure that you leave the door to the room open so the cat has regular access to his litterbox. The easiest way to create a house-soiling problem is to forget to leave that door open!

Kids, Meet the Kitty

If you have children, talk to them about how they should behave with their new pet well before her arrival. Explain that a cat is a living creature who will be part of their family, not a toy. They shouldn't manhandle, tease, yelled at, pinch, or poke her. Teach your children to approach and pet the cat gently and quietly. The children can even offer the cat a treat, or, if she seems willing, give her a toy to play with, such as a fake mouse or a teaser toy on the end of a wand. If the cat seems tentative, just let her investigate her new home while you and your children watch passively.

It's important to start the child/cat relationship off on the right foot; if your cat is frightened or mishandled on the first day, she won't forget it, and may never be open to contact with children again. Kittens will be more playful and open to contact, but remember that they are small and fragile, and can be easily hurt or panicked.

Encounters with Other Pets

Animals are curious and often concerned about protecting their territory, so it's a good idea to restrict any other pets you have temporarily when you first bring your new cat home. Allow your cat to live on her own, in a separate room for a day or two. Then, your other pets can have access to the rest of the home as usual; they will smell the new animal and be curious, but they won't be able to confront the cat directly.

Once all your other animals have become accustomed to the new cat's smell (and vice versa), consider briefly introducing them for ten or fifteen minutes at a time, *with the new cat safely in his travel crate.* Do this for the next few days, even placing the crate in the same room with the other animals while they are eating dinner. Finally, when it seems that everyone is calm and accustomed to the presence of the "new kid," begin letting the animals interact for brief periods of time without the use of the crate. Supervise, but be careful; if they fight, you could get scratched or bitten. (A cat bite or scratch can easily become infected.)

Realize that there will be territorial conflicts. Your pets will just have to work it out among themselves, and eventually they should. It might take a while for all of your animals to become best buds, so be patient. But they should at least begin to tolerate each other's presence after a few weeks.

Cat Tales: The Truth about Cats and Dogs

A kitten will have a better chance of bonding with a cat-friendly dog, but it still can be risky. If the dog is a puppy, or he was raised from puppyhood with cats, then you have a great chance of getting them to bond. Never get a new cat if you know your resident pets are aggressive toward other animals! You could end up with a badly injured kitty.

What to Do When Kitty Cries

It's almost a given that your new cat or kitten will feel confused and lonely at first. A kitten especially will miss her mother and siblings, and might even cry a lot because of it. This is sure to tug at your heartstrings, but don't worry; there are several things you can do to comfort your kitty.

- Keep her interested in her new environment. Have toys and other curious objects around for your kitty to play with and investigate. Often, something as simple as a brown paper bag or a large cardboard box will amuse a kitten for hours.

- Give your kitten as much attention and affection as she is willing to take, to fill the void left by her mother, siblings, or "buddies." Cuddle her, brush her, and talk to her in soft tones.

- Consider allowing your cat to sleep with you, or at least next to your bed on a bed of her own.

- Keep a radio on while you are gone; tune it into a talk radio station, and keep the volume low. This will help kitty to feel that she's not alone.

- Adopt more than one cat or kitten (preferably littermates). Two kitties will amuse each other while you are gone. This is the easiest way to keep kittens happy, and to prevent destructive behavior that results from boredom or loneliness.

Feline Psychology

To understand the cat's motivations and desires is to see into the feline psyche. If you want to raise a healthy, well-adjusted cat with whom you can forge a strong bond, you need to understand how she thinks, the ways in which she communicates, and what motivates her.

THE BARE NECESSITIES

The following things are basic necessities; when these needs are met, it makes for a happy, emotionally stable cat.

Food

Eating is, of course, an elemental drive for all creatures. Apart from the need to reproduce, there is probably no stronger motivation in the animal kingdom. In the wild, much of the cat's energies are directed toward hunting. Obtaining food is serious business; as such, it's an elemental part of the cat's psyche.

Though your domestic kitty has no need to fend for himself, his instinct to hunt and kill is still intact, just like his desire to eat. Those of you who allow your cats to go outdoors have, no doubt, received "gifts" from time to time, in the form of unfortunate little mouse or bird trophies dropped on the doorstep. This is your cat's way of proudly flaunting his hunting skills. But even if you have an indoor cat, this motivation to hunt will still affect many aspects of your cat's behavior. Even eight-week-old kittens love to stalk and pounce on toys—that's their way of expressing the instinctive desire to hunt.

Cat Tales: Stay Away from My Food!

Though much more prevalent in dogs, food aggression can be a problem with cats as well, particularly when a new cat is suddenly introduced into the established cat's domain. If yours is a multicat home, use more than one food dish to avoid this sort of squabbling.

Because food is such a strong motivator for cats, it can be used to shape feline behavior (this will be discussed in more detail later in the book).

Territory

Your kitty has the same basic territorial drives as a bobcat or a tiger. Though of no real value to the cat or us, these drives are nevertheless much in effect, even when cats don't go outside. Respect for this fact will help to foster a safe, happy environment for your cat. An ill-guided well wisher who impulsively brings a big dog, three cats, and a ferret into their six-year-old Persian's two-bedroom apartment knows nothing about the feline psyche, but will learn soon enough!

A domestic cat will stake out his territory by marking, scratching, or physically intimidating other cats. (These behaviors, when exhibited indoors, can be a problem; some solutions are presented later in this book.) You can minimize this territorial instinct by raising your kitty in the company of other animals, and also by providing enough food for all to be satiated. Nevertheless, cats will show territorial apprehensions when they are in the presence of unfamiliar animals or people.

Secure Environment

Cats don't like surprises and don't respond well to new, unusual, or unpredictable events. These things stress them out. For instance, if you regularly foster strange animals for short periods of time, it can be very upsetting to your kitty. It might even result in fighting and other displacement behaviors such as scratching furniture, marking, and soiling outside the litterbox. Likewise, when many different human guests visit your home, it can also confuse and upset your cat, who won't expect them. Remember, cats crave a predictable home life and aren't as socially outgoing as dogs. Steer clear of blaring music, raucous parties, and tail-pulling toddlers, and you'll have a happier cat!

Sex Drive

The instinct to procreate is strong in cats, as it is in all animals. Unless you get them spayed or neutered first, both males and females will begin to show a desire to mate by the time they are seven to ten months old. An unneutered male who is allowed outdoors will get into fights with other males and roam for days in search of a female in heat. If kept indoors he will be extremely vocal and will mark and scratch all over the home. An unspayed female will also cry and possibly mark in the home. She'll rub up against you and the floor incessantly, and wander around the home aimlessly waiting for you to let her outside. Which you should never do, because without question, an unspayed female wandering around outside *will* get pregnant, period. The answer to this dilemma is quite simple: Always neuter or spay your cats.

Nurturing

During kittenhood, interaction with the mother and littermates is crucial because it teaches the kitten about feline etiquette and relationships. It also helps to minimize antisocial or fear-aggressive tendencies later in life. This early nurturing period provides a kitten with an abiding love of maternal and sibling attention, and the kitten, in turn, usually transfers this love to her human family. It is the basis for most cats' desire for human contact, for they see us not as competing cats or masters, but as parental figures and siblings.

As such, domestic cats remain somewhat adolescent-minded when interacting with us. This part of their psyche differs from that of their wild cousins, who grow up quickly and do not usually maintain relations with parents or siblings. Cats who were not with their mothers and siblings for at least the first eight weeks of life can be aggressive toward other cats and timid around people later in life. Most cats who show an intense fear of unfamiliar humans probably left their litters too early, usually by the time they were four or five weeks old. It is important for cat parents to recognize the impact that good nurturing early in the kitten's life can have on their adult feline's psyche and emotional wellbeing.

Playtime

Play is possibly the most important developmental activity of kittenhood, and it greatly affects a cat's psychological and physiological development. Through play, a kitten's world becomes increasingly filled with interesting things to do. Kittens learn a rudimentary dominance hierarchy among themselves; though nothing like that of dogs, it does exist at this stage of development. They also learn to groom each other, a practice crucial to their human family later on because it teaches the cat to be tolerant of handling, brushing, and combing.

Play keeps the litter together and occupied while a cat mother is hunting, and it teaches proper social skills, including what is acceptable and improper, and how to "posture" with other kittens. Through play, kittens learn about the world around them by investigating their immediate environment; develop coordination and timing; bolster their sense of self-sufficiency; and sharpen hunting skills by climbing, chasing, stalking, and pouncing with littermates. Play also stimulates intellectual growth, both behaviorally and physiologically. An interesting, stimulating environment actually promotes the formation of neural pathways in a kitten's brain.

By twelve to fourteen weeks, kittens are less motivated to play and are ready to be independent and go out on their own. But a cat remembers play and will relive it through you, her owner.

Stimulation

All animals need intellectual and physical stimulation to remain emotionally healthy. Those isolated from any kind of input become antisocial, timid, and unbalanced. Humans left in solitary confinement are evidence of this. Cats are no different; the health of their psyches depends on a regular diet of interesting, stimulating things to do. All good cat parents should be mindful of this and provide their cat with companionship and plenty of diversions in the home, to prevent him from becoming bored and destructive.

Sleep

Cats sleep a lot—as much as fourteen to eighteen hours each day. Rather than sleeping straight through, however, cats usually take numerous naps. It is not clear just why cats need so much sleep, though it may have to do with their level of activity during waking hours. Kittens, especially, go full bore for hours and then zonk out for two-thirds of the day. The development of portions of the kitten's brain is also known to occur only during sleep.

Whatever the reason, understanding your cat's psyche means respecting her need to sleep undisturbed for somewhat lengthy periods, so make sure your kitty has a warm, comfy spot all her own. Just don't expect that she'll extend the same courtesy—if she's wide awake at 3:00 in the morning but you're sound asleep, that certainly won't deter her from meowing and pawing at you to play!

FELINE SMARTS

How smart is the domestic cat? That is a hard question to answer, because intelligence is not an easy concept to define. If we choose to use trainability as a barometer for intelligence, then the dog would certainly appear smarter than the cat. Dogs can learn to perform just about any behavior, if their trainer is clever enough and develops a strong relationship with the animal. But trainability is not the sole indicator of how smart an animal is.

Cat Tales: Basic Training

Cats are not pack animals, and do not recognize a leader in the same way dogs do. Because of this they don't always respond reliably to training. They are trainable, however, as you will learn later in this book. Cats continue to learn throughout their lives, but if you want to teach cats good habits and break them of bad habits, start training them when they are kittens.

Problem solving is probably a better indicator of intelligence, and cats are keen problem-solvers. They understand spatial problems better than dogs, owing to their ability to live in a more varied three-dimensional environment (dogs just can't flit up to the top of the fridge the way cats can). Cats do quite well in maze experiments, and they seem to retain knowledge for a very long time. For instance, if someone strikes a cat (something highly objectionable), the cat will retain the memory of the abuse seemingly forever and may never trust that person again.

The ability to adapt and flourish in different environments is yet another indicator of intellect. In that case, the domestic cat must have quite a head on her shoulders. Living and prospering in nearly every country in the world, cats can not only endure extremes of climate but can seemingly switch from domesticity to feral living at the flip of a coin. Most cats can easily survive without human mastery quite well, falling back on hunting instincts that have never really been abandoned during all the years of feline domesticity.

How Cats Learn

In order to better understand your cat's psyche, it is helpful to first understand just how a cat learns about his world.

Observation and Imitation

Cats don't operate purely on instinctive behavior—learned behavior widens their repertoire of possible responses, thereby improving chances for survival. Cats are good at learning specific behaviors by watching other cats, particularly their mothers. After watching his mother stalk and catch a mouse, for example, a kitten or young cat will mimic that behavior and eventually master it. Learning by observation works best in kittens and young cats. Older cats can learn as well, but it may take longer.

Trial and Error

All animals, including humans and cats, can learn by accident. For example, if a human baby cries, she quickly learns that she will get her parents' attention. Likewise, a kitten quickly learns that she can't get to an abandoned sandwich on the kitchen counter by jumping straight up from the kitchen floor. And so she learns to use a chair as a transitional step to get up to the counter and into a whole mess of trouble. You can bet that cat won't forget the chair trick anytime soon.

Conditioned Response

Two types of conditioning can affect cats' behavior. With *classical conditioning*, a cat learns on a subliminal level to perform a certain behavior when given a certain stimulus. Pavlov's dogs are the perfect example; they were conditioned to salivate to the sound of a bell, always rung right before food was provided. Salivation was an automatic response. Likewise, as most cat owners know, a kitty will come running into the kitchen anytime he hears the sound of a can opener. That's classical conditioning at work.

With *operant conditioning*, a cat learns to repeat a certain behavior that is followed by some sort of reward (usually food), or conversely learns to avoid a behavior that is followed by some unpleasant consequence. This is the main technique used to train cats to perform tricks and to stop undesirable behaviors such as eating houseplants or scratching furniture. Good behaviors are reinforced; unwanted behaviors are either replaced with more desirable ones or averted through use of an unpleasant (though harmless) consequence each time the cat acts up. So, for example, as positive reinforcement you could reward your cat with a treat for sitting in front of you. And for negative reinforcement (or aversion), you might spray the cat with a squirt bottle of water whenever he attempted to chew on a houseplant.

CAT COMMUNICATION

Cats express their feelings, intentions, desires, and attitudes through a complex mix of vocal, posturing, and marking behaviors. The sounds that they make, the body postures they assume, and the places where they eliminate all play a role in telling the world how they feel and what they want.

Body Language

Body language does play a significant role in cat-to-cat communication. A cat's tail is a good indicator of what is going on in his head. A straight-up tail with a bit of movement to it usually denotes an alert, contented attitude: This is a cat who is ready to be friendly yet is actively curious about his environment. If the cat is lying down and his tail is relaxed, then he is in an easygoing mood. If the tail lowers slightly and lashes back and forth, it usually means the cat is worried or angry. And nothing says "Don't mess with me" like a downward, arched tail.

A cat's ears are great indicators of mood. When held in an erect, forward position, the cat is usually in a happy, curious mood. When the openings of the ears are rotated forward, it means that the cat is on the alert. If the ears face backward, it normally denotes worry; this cat may be ready for confrontation. If the ears are erect with the openings facing backward, it usually means, "I'm going to kick your butt." Finally, when a cat's ears are plastered flat against her head, it means she's frightened and might be ready to defend herself or run away.

Cat Tales: Wagging or Not?

As a general rule, cats and dogs are complete opposites with regard to tail movement. A wagging tail on a dog usually means, "Hi, I'm happy you're near me"; the same movement in a cat's tail means, "You worry me, so hit the highway." The tail of an angry or frightened cat will also bristle.

A cat who rubs her body against you or kneads her paws into you is being affectionate and somewhat possessive. Kneading is a behavior left over from kittenhood, when little ones knead at their mother's nipples to stimulate milk production. When your cat does this, it's a sure sign that she thinks of you as her mommy. Your cat's gently touching you with her paw also denotes affection, but a swat with that same paw means, "It's time to back off!"

Cats' eyes also help to communicate intentions. If your feline stares intently at someone or something, it usually means he's either very interested or somewhat threatened. If a staring cat begins to blink or avert his eyes, it generally signals submission. A cat who is relaxed and calm usually has his eyelids slightly lowered, whereas a fearful cat's eyes will be wide open with pupils dilated.

A feline's entire body posture can signify a mood or emotion. If the cat's back is arched and all his hair is bristling, you know he's scared and ready to rumble. Cats who rub their bodies against you are normally happy and content. If your cat flops over on her back it can mean she's playful and wants a tummy rub. Just watch out if her paws are brandished in the air—it could mean "stay away."

A cat's face also communicates emotion. Constant tongue flicking denotes worry, whereas an open-mouthed pant can mean exhaustion, sickness, or fear. If a male cat has a strange sneering look on his face while panting, it may mean that he is scenting a female in heat and is therefore sexually aroused.

Vocalization

Cats convey information to others through audible signals. Some breeds (the Siamese, for example) are more vocal than others. All, however, exhibit the standard cat sounds at one time or another. That famous "meow" usually means a cat wants something, is confused, or else is mildly miffed and wants you to do something about it. When cats "chirp," or grunt softly, it usually means, "Welcome home, I'm glad to see you." Growling, hissing, and snarling usually mean a cat is really ticked off or angry; give her some space when you hear any of these! Crying typically means a cat is scared or worried and might be in need of comfort and reassurance. However, the wailing cry of a female denotes the pain endured during the mating process. It's a sound no one appreciates or soon forgets. The familiar purr, though not a true vocalization, usually denotes contentment, but can at times mean the cat is worried.

Marking

Marking is an effective way for cats to communicate with each other instead of coming to blows. When cats mark, they identify and claim territory as their own. Though it is more common in male than female cats, both sexes will mark. The male cat's urine contains a fatty ingredient that allows it to adhere to objects and surfaces and last even through a rainfall or two. When another male comes by, he can immediately discern that he has entered another male's territory; at that point he can politely retreat or try to claim the spot as his own by marking over it. This action will, of course, provoke more marking behavior by the original male, and perhaps lead to open hostilities between the two.

Cats also use feces to mark territory. In the wild, dominant cats who are competing for territory often do not bury their waste; only smaller or more submissive cats do so, a way of ensuring that dominant cats do not feel challenged. Burying waste is also a way of preventing a predator from tracking the cat and eating it! Your house cat buries his waste not only out of hygiene; he's also saying that he recognizes you as the dominant cat in the home. Conversely, one reason why your cat might choose not to use his litterbox may be that he considers himself to be dominant over you. There are others reasons for this nasty habit, though, and these will be discussed later in this book.

Cat Tales: The Unpredictable Feline

Although we can expound to no end about the cat psyche and, perhaps, explain it in a general sense, in the end, there is no foolproof way to predict these things. Every feline is an individual—some are shy while others are bold and sassy. As your cat's trusted companion and caregiver, you will learn to key into her individual personality in order to truly understand exactly what she wants and how she is feeling.

Scratching is another way cats mark territory. In addition to leaving glandular secretions from between the toes, the scratches left on trees, fences, or (unfortunately) furniture are visible markers of territorial boundaries. Both wild and domestic cats tend to pick a few choice scratching spots and then use them over and over again; this is one of the reasons why breaking a pet's bad scratching habit is so difficult.

Cats mark by other means, too. They have scent glands on the chin, around the eyes, below the ears, on the sides of the forehead, in and around the anus, between the toes, and at the base of the tail. Cats use these glands to further define territory, to inform other cats of their sexual conditions and intentions, or to release stress.

Friendly greetings between cats also involve some exchange of scent secretions, usually from rubbing each other with the glands on the head and face. This action plus the offering up of the anal areas for mutual inspection is normally interpreted as a sign of acceptance and respect (as odd as that sounds to us). So, when your cat greets you by rubbing her head all over you, it's not just because she wants to make contact. It is a gesture of acceptance as well as a way of saying "You are mine."

Feeding and Grooming Your Cat

How often do kittens need to eat, and how much food should you give them? What's the best way to catch your kitty for nail-cutting time? And is it really possible to brush a cat's teeth? So many questions, and so much to think about when caring for a cat. This chapter will take you through the ins and outs of essential care.

FOOD FOR YOUR FELINE

There are three types of commercially available cat food you can choose.

Canned Food

Canned foods are normally highly nutritious and have a long shelf life. They are more expensive than dry food, however, and tend to be about 70 percent water. If you decide on a supermarket or pet shop brand of canned food, make sure it has your vet's approval. Also be prepared to clean your cat's teeth on a fairly regular basis because canned food is soft and nonabrasive.

Dry Food

Dry food is more economical than canned food. It also stays fresher longer in your cat's bowl, making it a better choice if you leave food out all day. Because it's abrasive, dry food will help to keep your cat's teeth cleaner. Consider opting for higher-quality pet shop brands instead of cheaper but less nutritious supermarket foods, which can have higher amounts of preservatives and ash, and lower amounts of essential nutrients such as fatty acids and taurine. As always, consult your vet when in doubt.

Semimoist

Semimoist foods are often used as an alternative to canned. They are lighter and easier to store, and very palatable to most cats. These foods tend to be expensive, however, and often contain preservatives, artificial coloring, binders, and sugar. In addition, they do not help clean the cat's teeth.

Combo Platter

Many owners decide to feed their cats dry food and supplement daily with some canned food to increase the available amounts of protein and fatty acids. This is not only a less expensive alternative to a canned-only diet, it will ensure that a growing kitten gets ample protein into her system without developing tooth decay early on.

FEEDING YOUR KITTEN

Up to six or eight months, a kitten should eat at least twice a day. A very young kitten (ten to eighteen weeks) might do better with three or even four meals per day. In order to meet nutritional requirements, you must give a kitten two to three times the amount of food (on a per-pound of body weight basis) you would give an adult. Kittens need more protein, too. Therefore, it's important to select a food specifically designed for growing kittens.

Whatever food you choose to feed your young feline, make sure that it is specifically designed for a kitten. Feeding adult cat food (or dog food) to a kitten can stunt growth and lead to other physiological problems.

FEEDING YOUR ADULT CAT

Though adult cats require a high amount of protein in their diet compared to dogs or humans, they still need less than kittens. An adult cat who is fed kitten food may, over time, develop kidney or liver problems. When your cat is between eight to ten months old, switch to an adult cat food that meets your vet's approval. Consider feeding your adult cat twice per day at regular times. This will ensure your cat develops a hunger drive, or "appetite," an important aid not only in maintaining health but in training as well. Vary the amount you feed according to the cat's weight and level of activity; a lazy, relaxed animal needs less food than a hyperactive one.

Cat Tales: Weighing In

Get into the habit of weighing your cat once a month, to track any losses or gains. Ask your vet what an ideal weight for your cat would be, then try to keep as close to it as possible. To weigh your cat, simply pick her up, weigh both of you on a home scale, then weigh yourself and subtract this amount from the combined amount.

As cats age, their metabolism slows down. Your older cat may need to begin eating a lower-calorie "senior" food in order to maintain a healthy weight.

Also, be on the lookout for constipation in an older cat, caused by reduced motility in the intestines, decreased liver function, and an increasing inability to absorb nutrients. Your vet may recommend adding more fiber to your cat's diet. Commercially available fiber supplements can be used, as can oat bran. Adding one-half teaspoon of olive oil once each day to your cat's food can also help.

The Benefits of Scheduled Feedings

To a cat, food is one of the only behavioral motivators. A cat who gets hungry regularly and predictably can be motivated to do many clever things in exchange for a choice tidbit at the right time.

Most owners leave food out for their cats all the time; this causes the cat to eat small amounts throughout the day instead of one or two scheduled meals. This works to *reduce* a cat's desire for food. The cat is never really hungry, and isn't as motivated to do anything for a food reward.

Cat Tales: Caloric Requirements

The typical ten-pound cat needs approximately 300 calories per day to remain healthy, while the fifteen-pound bruiser (perhaps a Maine coon cat) needs around 400. These numbers will vary with the age, breed, and lifestyle of the cat, of course; consult your vet if in doubt about how much your cat should eat.

Having a hunger drive and satisfying it is a natural way of life for a cat, so it's a good idea to feed your cat at regular times during the day instead of leaving food out all the time. It's best to feed your cat twice per day at precise times, perhaps in the morning before you go to work, then in the evening when you come home. Then, your cat will anticipate the arrival of food at a specific time instead of lazily picking at his chow throughout the day, and you can harness his hunger drive to teach him new things and modify undesirable behaviors.

Of course, it's not absolutely a must that you feed your cat at specific times if that doesn't work for you. You can free-feed your cat without any ill effects, as long as you make sure she's not overeating. Cats who pick all day can become overweight if their owners continually refill their food dish whenever it's empty. If you do free-feed, pay attention to how much you're giving your cat and how much she's eating, so that she maintains her proper weight.

FAT CATS

Normally, cats should have a thin layer of fat underneath the skin, but you should still be able to feel their ribs. The typical house cat should not weigh more than twelve to fifteen pounds, unless it is a larger breed. Don't let your cat pork out. Overfeeding can lead to an overweight cat. Obesity, in turn, can contribute to a number of health problems, including diabetes, heart disease, respiratory stress, and structural injuries.

Cats are considered obese if they are 15 to 20 percent over their ideal body weight (determined by your vet). If your cat is obese, you can correct the problem by following these suggestions:

1. Switch from free-feeding to scheduled feedings.

2. Cut back 20 percent on your cat's daily food intake or feed him a "senior" cat food, which has fewer calories per unit volume. Then the cat will eat the same amount but take in fewer calories.

3. Ensure that your overweight cat gets more exercise. Play with him, teach him to walk on a leash, or let him frolic with another animal he knows and trusts.

4. Do not give a fat cat too many treats between meals. If you are using treats for training purposes, just subtract that amount of food from the cat's total allotted food for the day.

5. Reduce the amount of food accordingly after your cat is neutered if necessary, because neutering can slow metabolism slightly.

6. Do not indulge your obese cat when he comes begging for food.

7. Stay firm when it comes to feeding an adopted stray extra food. Strays who previously had to fight for food often become pudgy when unlimited food is suddenly available. Their hardships have caused them to develop an incredible hunger drive; be tough and avoid giving them so much food they become blimps and float away.

FINICKY CATS

If you have a finicky cat, take heart. Here are some things you can do to correct the problem.

1. Feed your cat at regular intervals to restore her natural hunger drive. Then, she'll look forward to mealtime and won't be as finicky. This will also help your cat to learn desired behaviors in exchange for a well-timed food reward.

2. Feed a severely underweight cat dry food with some canned food to increase caloric intake.

3. Weigh your cat each month and keep track of any changes. Adjust food intake accordingly to maintain proper weight.

4. Limit your cat's stress levels as much as possible by sticking to the status quo. This will help to prevent abnormal eating habits.

5. If you have more than one cat, don't let one hog down the other's food in addition to his own. Consider feeding your cats in

different locations to ensure that each gets the right amount and is given enough time to finish.

If your cat suddenly becomes a very finicky eater or stops eating completely, see your vet. There might be some medical problem that needs to be identified and treated. For example, an underactive or overactive thyroid gland can affect eating habits, as can allergies, diabetes, and intestinal blockages.

Coat Care

Unlike dogs, who usually loved to be touched and groomed at any time, cats can be more skittish about this sort of handling. Start grooming your kitten as soon as she comes home, so that she'll accept being brushed, combed, and handled on a daily basis. Grooming helps to remove loose hairs from the cat's coat that can cause hairballs in the stomach when a cat licks himself clean. Though normally regurgitated or passed by the cat, they can sometimes cause intestinal blockages that necessitate veterinary assistance.

Talk quietly, praise her, and perhaps reward her with a treat at the end of the session. As your cat gets used to being brushed, she may look forward to the ritual.

Trimming Nails

You should start trimming your cat's nails when he is very young. Most cats aren't too happy having their feet handled, so if you have an adult cat who has never had his nails clipped before or if clipping makes you too nervous, it might be a good idea to have a professional groomer do the work for you every few months.

Here is the procedure for trimming your cat's nails:

1. Every day for one month, while petting your kitten, briefly and gently handle each paw. Massage each between your thumb and forefinger, exposing the nails as you do. Gradually make brief, casual contact with each nail, then heartily praise your little one and reward her with a treat or a toy.

2. Once your kitten is thoroughly accustomed to having her feet and nails rubbed, begin lightly touching each nail with the clippers during the handling procedure. Do not trim anything yet. Just desensitize your kitten to the metallic feel of the clippers. Continue this for two weeks; praise and reward her.

3. After your kitten has learned to accept having her nails touched, try to clip one or two casually. Don't take off more than a six-teenth of an inch of nail! Just get the kitten used to the action, and learn how much pressure it takes to trim a kitten's nails. You have to build your skills and confidence before cutting all the nails in earnest. Always be conservative with how much you trim off; trimming off too much will cut into the quick, a visible blood vessel running down the center of each nail. Cut only the over-grown tip of each nail; otherwise, if you do cut the quick, the nail will bleed. And if you hurt your kitten, she'll lose trust in you.

Cat Tales: Quick Nail Fix

Keep some styptic powder or flour on hand in case you do cut to the quick when trimming kitty's nails. Either one of these powders will quickly stop the bleeding if gently pressed into the nail tip.

4. Once you and the kitten are comfortable with trimming one or two nails, trim one entire paw. Since trimming the nails on all four paws in one session will probably make your kitten fidgety and nervous, try one paw each day. Remember to praise and reward the little tyke after each session.

CLEANING EARS

It's important to train your cat to tolerate having his ears inspected and cleaned periodically. Indoor cats need this less than outdoor cats, but all owners should be able to check their cat's ears. Here's what to do:

1. While stroking your kitten's head, casually rub his ears, then gently rub your pinkie tip around the inside of the ear. Do this with both ears, then praise and reward. Do this for a week before moving on. Make sure you inspect the ears for dirt, wax buildup, and parasites.

2. While stroking the kitten's head and ears, gently touch the inside of each ear with a dry cotton swab for a few seconds. Praise and reward afterward. Repeat this for several sessions.

3. Dip the swab in mineral oil and repeat step two; extend the period of contact. Clean off any dirt or wax on the inside of each ear—be casual and quick. Then dry each ear with the dry end of the swab. Praise the kitten and reward him with food.

4. Continue to inspect and handle the cat's ears at least once a week, even if they are clean, so your cat accepts this behavior. If done properly and regularly, your cat will learn to trust your handling more and more.

Cat Tales: Be Careful with Cotton Swabs

Never stick a cotton swab down into your cat's ear canal; clean only the visible outer areas. If you see dirt or wax deep inside the canal, take your kitty to the vet. Also see your vet if your cat's ears are continually dirty or if they have a discharge—it could be a sign of infection.

CARING FOR TEETH AND GUMS

Over time, deposits of plaque can form on your cat's teeth, mostly on the molars and premolars. If tartar, a harder substance, builds on cats' teeth, it can lead to gum disease and tooth loss—not to mention bad kitty breath. Once tartar buildup is significant, your vet will have to clean it off using an ultrasonic device, with the cat under general anesthesia.

In addition to feeding your cat a mostly dry-food diet, you can clean your cat's teeth on a monthly basis to remove plaque. Remember, start young, because adult cats won't relish this procedure!

1. Gently rub your cat's gums and teeth with a finger while you pet and praise her. Be casual and confident, and don't rub for more than five or ten seconds at first. Gradually build up until you can cover all of the cat's teeth and gums. (Getting all the way into the back might be difficult with your finger, so don't push it.)

2. After the kitten is used to your finger, switch to a dry cotton swab and continue the procedure. The swab will allow you easier access to the molars. Continue this once each day for a few days.

3. Wet the swab with warm salt water and repeat the procedure. Continue for a few days before moving on. Make sure you use enough pressure to remove any loose food on the teeth or at the gum line. Praise and reward the kitten afterward.

4. If you'd like, you can then apply a bit of baking soda to the moistened swab, or use a feline toothpaste.

Look for chipped or loose teeth while brushing. Also examine the gums for inflammation or bleeding. If you see any of this, call your vet.

Teaching Basic Behaviors

Y ou'll have to tackle some basic training if you want a feline who grows up to be a well-adjusted, well-behaved member of your family. Foster an atmosphere of mutual trust and cooperation, and things will go more smoothly. For starters, establish some basic behavior guidelines for your cat to follow. Your cat won't just magically know what these guidelines are and how to follow them; you'll have to teach those things. Once basic behaviors are in place, you and your kitty will better understand each other's role in your relationship, and you'll both appreciate each other more fully.

LEAD HER TO THE LITTERBOX

As already explained, most cats have an instinctive desire to bury their waste, and by the time you bring your kitty home, she should have this behavior down fairly well (unless she was separated too early from her mother and never learned this).

Once you show your cat where the litterbox is, it shouldn't take the little one long to get the idea. When your cat uses the litterbox properly, always praise her. Just don't be a pest and hang around each time she does her business—cats like their privacy!

Stick to these rules to ensure your cat uses her litterbox regularly:

1. Decide on the best location for the litterbox, and then keep it there. Cats can become confused if you suddenly move the box to a far-off spot, and this could lead to accidents.

2. Put the litterbox in a quiet spot where your cat won't be bothered by humans or other animals. If you have a cat-friendly dog in the home, keep the litterbox outside of the dog's domain, or prop open the door to the room just enough so the cat can slip through, but not the dog.

3. Stick with the same brand of litter. Cats get used to the texture and odor; if you change that suddenly, your cat might refuse to use her box and opt for your flowerpots, closets, or dirty laundry piles instead.

Cat Tales: Litter Switch

If for some reason you must change litter brands, do so gradually, by mixing the new litter with the old litter over the course of three to four weeks. Switching over too quickly could make for mishaps.

4. Keep the box clean! The most common reason a cat won't use his box is because it's loaded with waste. Scoop out waste every day, possibly twice a day if two cats are using one box. Completely change the litter at least once a week if you use clay litter; you may change it less frequently if you use crystals. Just be sure to read the instructions and clean according to the suggested schedule.

TRAVEL TIME

Whether you're traveling in an airplane with your cat or going to the vet by car, you need to be able to get her in a travel crate. Start crate training when your cat is young. Pick her up, stroke her gently, then place her into the carrier and close the door. After a few minutes, take the cat out, praise her, and give her a treat. Practice regularly, increasing the time your cat stays in the crate as you go along. Once you have worked up to fifteen minutes or so, put the cat in the crate, carry her out to the car, and go for a short ride. As always, praise and reward her when you get home.

Your cat might not be so keen on the idea of getting into her crate. If she senses you are preparing for a trip, or you make the mistake of showing her the crate before it's time to leave, she could hide on you. Stay calm and quiet during crate round up; if you're nervous, your cat will pick up on it, and that will make matters worse. Instead, simply grab your cat by the scruff of the neck and guide her into the crate, reassuring her in a soft, soothing voice if she cries while in there.

Do Some Socializing

One of the most important parts of successful pet parenting is doing all that you can to ensure your cat will be confident, calm, and friendly around people. There is nothing worse than a cat who hisses, scratches, and bites guests, family members, or the veterinarian, simply because that person tried to pet, examine, or move the little fur ball off the sofa.

Several factors determine an animal's level of sociability:

Species: Cats as a species are usually shier and less outgoing than dogs, and they will not be as tolerant of strangers who insist on handling them.

Genetics: Some cats are predisposed to being more timid or aloof than others. This is largely determined by their parents' genetic makeup; if they are overly wary of strangers, chances are their offspring will be, too. You can help your cat to overcome these traits through training, but they cannot be eliminated.

Breed: Certain cat breeds tend to be more sociable than others. A Persian, for example, is usually more aloof than a Siamese.

Time spent with mother and littermates: As previously explained, cats who leave their mothers and littermates before seven or eight weeks are more likely to be timid or antisocial. Those who spend adequate time interacting with mother and siblings will be more confident and socially aware. With training, patience, and plenty of love, however, you can often help a timid cat to overcome this.

Past experiences: A cat or kitten who has been abused or neglected tends to be less sociable than one who enjoyed good treatment from the start.

With proper socialization, cats can grow up to be confident and interactive, even when they meet new people. Socialize your kitty as much as possible, right from the start. As soon as your kitten is settled into your home, begin to have regular handling, petting, and grooming sessions with him. Play with toys together as well; kittens love to play, and they learn to trust their playmates—namely, you.

Cat Tales: Give Yourself a Tail!

If your kitty is eager to play but you need to get things done around the house, try tying or clipping a long piece of yarn to the back of your pants, and watch how fast your cat will be chasing your "tail." This might sound like a silly idea, but it works wonders: It helps you to socialize and bond with your kitty.

Invite friends over, although not all at once, and practice the same techniques. Be sure to expose your kitten to a variety of people. Include men, women, and responsible children. Just make sure they don't roughhouse or get too loud—they could frighten your kitty. The more people your kitten bonds with and trusts, the better.

The More Cats the Merrier?

You have to be particularly mindful when you bring a new cat home to other cats. Remember, the single best way to get cats to interact peaceably is to raise them together from kittenhood, which is why it's best to bring two littermates, or another kitten of comparable age, home at the same time. They'll bond together through play and develop their own sibling understanding of how to interact with each other.

If you bring a kitten into your home with an older cat or cats, remember that adult cats are extremely territorial. Your resident feline has claimed your home as his territory, and he won't want to share it with some young upstart! When you do introduce a new kitten or cat into another cat's domain, pay as much—if not more—attention to the resident cat, especially when the new kid is around. This will reassure your resident cat that even though he's no longer the only game in town, he'll still get plenty of love, attention, cuddling, and stroking. Make sure all the cats know there is enough affection to go around, and it will help to minimize conflicts.

Dog Days

The same "sibling camaraderie" rule applies to socializing cats with dogs. Pups and kittens raised together from a young age often become great lifelong friends. If either animal is an adult at the time of their meeting, proceed carefully. You know your pet's personality best. If, for example, you have an aggressive, less-than-friendly dog, a cat might not be the best idea. On the other hand, a dog who is laid back, affectionate, and easy-going might take to a cat just fine.

Particularly if an adult dog has had exposure to cats for her entire life, she should have little problem adapting to a new cat or kitten. Nevertheless, supervise them carefully for the first month or two, and make sure they are getting along well before you leave them alone together in the same part of the house. *Never* leave a young kitten alone with a dog, however friendly the pooch might be. Even in play a dog could accidentally hurt a tiny feline.

Socializing Fearful Felines

If you have adopted a timid, fearful kitten or adult cat, do not prematurely attempt to have your friends handle, pet, or groom her; your cat might bite or scratch because she's scared. Instead, simply have one person at a time visit your home for several hours, with your cat present. Your cat will probably run and hide at first, but have each person stick around long enough for her to come out slowly to investigate. Your visitors shouldn't try to follow the cat around or pick her up—just having them there, near you while your cat is present, is enough. Give your guests some yummy treats to drop near your cat each time she comes near. This way, your cat will build positive associations with friends and family members who visit.

Don't expect an extremely fearful adult cat to become a social butterfly. This sort of cat might never be comfortable allowing lots of different people to pick him up or play with him. Respect your cat's boundaries if this is the case, and encourage guests to wait for the cat to come to them. Over time, as your cat sees that these strangers are not out to hurt him, he might be more accepting of visitors.

CONDITIONED RESPONSE

During the first few months with your new cat, begin to teach him about positive reinforcement for desirable behaviors. It's easy—simply praise and reward the cat for proper behavior. If he doesn't put up a fuss when you brush him, stroke him and reward him with a treat. When he responds to his name, do the same. If he's sociable with other animals and people, reward him for that, too.

Many people have the wrong idea that cats have no interest in being taught, but this is far from true. Cats are smart, and they deserve to be mentally stimulated just as much as dogs. Chapter 9 will discuss how you can correct undesirable behaviors; right now, just concentrate on rewarding your kitten for behaving properly and understanding the consequences of his actions. By teaching your cat these things, you will expand his intellect and make your life a lot easier, because you'll be motivating him to *think* about his behavior instead of just reacting to stimuli.

NAME THAT KITTY

It's important to teach your cat to recognize and respond to her name. This will expand her intellect and strengthen the bond between you. Name recognition also sets the tone for future training because it introduces the cat to the principle of conditioned response, and positive/negative reinforcement for behaviors.

While you have your cat in front of you or on your lap, pet her immediately after saying her name. Do this each time you pet her or give her a treat. If you practice from the time your cat is young, eventually she'll learn to recognize it and will associate the sound of her name with something pleasant, which will make her more attentive to you.

TEACHING "COME"

It is easier to teach your cat to come to you than you might think! Often, people do this inadvertently; many cats automatically race into the kitchen whenever they hear the sound of the can opener or the treat bag rattling.

In addition to stimulating your cat's mind, learning the "come" command strengthens her social bond with you and other family members. "Come" can also be used as a distraction behavior. When you see your cat is about to do something she shouldn't—like dig into a flower pot or scratch the couch—instead of yelling at her or squirting her with water, you can opt for calling her to you and rewarding her. Then your cat will forget about her mischief in favor of getting petted and fed. Here's how to teach "come":

1. Keep your cat on a regular feeding schedule, as discussed earlier. This way, she'll have a well-defined hunger drive, the basis for teaching all tricks.

2. Buy a "clicker" training device—most pet stores sell them. The clicker creates a sudden, percussive noise that really grabs the cat's attention.

3. For one month, whenever you put food in your cat's dish, click the clicker repeatedly until she comes. Pet her, say "good," then leave her alone to enjoy her meal. Do this religiously, at feeding time only.

Cat Tales: Know When to Quit

When training "come" or any other behavior, never overwork your cat. Stop your training session when the cat has performed a task perfectly one time. Remember, cats get bored with too much repetition!

4. Right before dinnertime, stand within a few feet of your cat. With a great treat in one hand and the clicker in the other, click while holding out the treat. Your cat should come right over for the treat. Practice once each day, while continuing to click at feeding. As the cat catches on, gradually increase your distance, until, after a few weeks, you can click from another room and your cat will come to you.

This behavior should always be rewarded with food. Always say "good" to praise your cat when giving her the food reward.

WALKING ON A HARNESS AND LEASH

Everyone deserves a chance to stop and smell the roses sometimes—kitties included. Walking on a harness and leash is a safe, responsible way of letting your curious little creature enjoy the great outdoors.

Cat Tales: Harness Your Cat

Always attach the leash to a harness instead of a collar. This way, your cat won't be able to slip out of it if panicked. The harness also takes the pulling pressure off of your cat's neck—something that panics many cats.

Before training your cat to walk on a leash, there are a few things to keep in mind:

1. Teach this behavior while your cat is young. Few adult cats will tolerate wearing a harness and being attached to a leash.

2. Develop a strong sense of trust with your cat before attempting to walk her on a leash. Some cats are timid or nervous about trying this, even as kittens. If so, don't force her to comply. Patience is the watchword—take your time.

3. Keep things quiet. Never take your cat out on a leash in a busy area with lots of pedestrian and car traffic, startling noises, dogs, or hectic, unpredictable activity. Your cat might panic if she feels threatened, resulting in stress and possible injury. Only walk your cat in quiet, predictable areas, preferably in the backyard or on a peaceful residential street.

4. End your walk if your cat ever resists or panics. Never continue any behavior that upsets the cat.

5. Keep your cat's collar and identification tag on, in case she gets loose.

Invest in a leash and an adjustable harness when your cat is fourteen to sixteen weeks old, or after she has had all mandatory vaccinations. The leash should be four to five feet long and made of the lightest, thinnest material possible.

Here are the steps for teaching your cat to walk outside on a leash. (Practice in the safety of your own home before going outside.)

1. Don't put the harness and leash on your cat at first. Keep them next to her food dish for a week, or treat it as one of her toys. Encourage her to investigate, paw at it, and feel at ease around it.

2. Once your cat becomes accustomed to seeing the harness, pick her up and stroke her gently while sitting on the sofa. Stroke the cat with the harness a few times, so she gets used to the feel of it on her body. Do this for several days, praising the cat and rewarding her with a treat after each session.

3. Read the instructions and then gently put the harness on your cat during one of the above sessions. Take your time, and stop if the kitten gets nervous. Make sure the harness is loose. Reward your kitten with a treat, so that she associates the harness with something good. Do not move on until the kitten is relaxed when wearing the harness.

4. Increase the time that your kitten wears the harness, up to about twenty minutes, or the time that an outside excursion might last.

5. Once your kitten can comfortably wear the harness indoors for twenty minutes, clip on a light leash. Praise and reward the cat with food. Eventually, stand up and encourage the kitten to walk around the room. Use a toy to coax her if needed. Don't let go of the leash. Keep the leash loose as you follow her around the room, to minimize the tension the kitten feels. Work on this for a minute or two at first.

6. Gradually let the kitten experience a small amount of intermittent leash tension. Slowly increase this until some tension does not panic the kitten. *Never* pull hard on the leash, or yank the kitten around. Take at least a week to desensitize the kitten to leash tension.

7. Walk your kitten around the home once each day until she grows accustomed to it for longer periods of time. Remember to reward her during these walks. By this stage she should be relaxed and confident, but back off whenever she becomes resistant.

8. Take the kitten into a quiet yard, then let her investigate while on the harness and leash. Follow her around and keep leash tension to a minimum. Work for a few minutes, reward her, then go back inside. Gradually increase time spent outside, eventually encouraging the kitten to walk back inside on her own.

9. If the kitten is confident, walk her on a quiet residential street for a few minutes. Avoid hectic or dangerous situations!

10. Take your kitten out once each day. Always bring plenty of treats with you, and offer them liberally throughout the walk. Never let go of the leash!

Cat Tales: Don't Force the Situation

Never punish or scold your cat for not performing a behavior. Punishing a cat almost always results in a major loss of trust. Cats should not—and cannot—be forced to do anything. Build a strong relationship with your cat, earn her trust, and make her want to respond to training.

Once you and your feline have mastered the basic behaviors in this chapter, you'll be on your way to establishing a strong relationship. No relationship is problem-free, however; the next chapter will show you how to minimize your cat's inappropriate behaviors.

Troubleshooting Behavior Problems

"Proper behavior" is a relative concept. After all, just because your cat is not acting the way you want him to in your home doesn't mean he's behaving improperly for a cat. Marking and scratching are completely natural behaviors in the wild, but they're improper in the home because we deem them so. That said, as head of your household, you determine what is proper and improper behavior, and then apply those standards to your cats. In this chapter, you'll learn some straightforward ways to reduce or eliminate some of the most common feline behavior flaws.

Before you try to correct your cat's bad behaviors, visit your vet for a kitty checkup. Many odd behaviors that appear suddenly are the result of a physical problem and can be corrected through medical attention. Remember: medical first, behavioral second. You just might eliminate a bad behavior and possibly save your cat's life in the process. (Common feline illnesses will be discussed in Chapter 11.)

MESSING IN THE HOUSE

Urinating and defecating outside of the litterbox is far and away the most common behavioral problem in cats. First, determine if your cat is improperly eliminating to mark his territory. You'll have to catch the cat in the act. If the cat is squatting, then he or she is urinating, not marking (true for males and females). When cats mark, they remain standing, backing up to their target surface. Also, spraying usually involves less urine than does elimination, and will often be directed up on some vertical surface. Sprayed urine smells worse, because it's mixed with pheromones (glandular secretions). Marking through defecation is rare and will occur indoors only if a cat's indoor "core" territory is blatantly challenged.

The Litterbox Is the Culprit

If you have ruled out a medical problem, there are other possible causes and solutions.

A dirty litterbox might be the prime culprit. Owners who allow their cat's litterbox to fill up with waste are just asking for trouble. Keep the litterbox as clean as possible, consider getting an extra one if you have more than one cat, change litter frequently, and wash the box thoroughly.

Cat Tales: Neutralize Odors

You must thoroughly clean the area where a cat has improperly eliminated, and then treat it with an "odor neutralizer" to get rid of the smell of the cat's waste. Otherwise, the odor will attract the cat and cause repeated accidents.

Stick with a particular brand of litter and keep the box in the same spot at all times. Even going to a different style of litterbox can throw a cat into a tizzy. Remember, cats are finicky and set in their ways. The more static their environment, the happier they will be.

(See Chapters 5 and 8 for more details on litterbox problems.)

Too Close for Comfort

Cats will not eliminate near where they eat or sleep. If you have placed the litterbox too close to either of these places, that could be the root of your problem. Make sure the box is located as far as possible from both of these coveted areas. Also avoid placing the box too close to lots of noise or activity—inside or out of the house. If you have to relocate your cat's litterbox in order to correct any of these circumstances, do so gradually, and show the cat where it is.

Movin' Out

Relocating to a different home can be traumatic for a cat. Suddenly, with no warning, everything looks different, there are all sorts of new and unfamiliar smells everywhere, and your cat doesn't even recognize the lay of the land. A move to strange new territory is a serious matter to cats! Your cat needs to learn about her new home before she can be comfortable with it.

When moving to a new home, make sure you bring as much of the old furnishings, carpets, cat toys, and other items as you can. These things all contain the smell of your old home, and this will ease your cat somewhat. If your cat begins to have house-soiling problems immediately after moving to a new place, you may need to confine her to one room for a while when you're not home, until she calms down and gets used to the smell of the new place. Put the litterbox in one corner of the room, but don't put the cat's food in there; it will be too close to the litterbox. Instead, feed the cat in another room when you come home.

If the problem continues, reduce the cat's "living" area by using a wire mesh crate that's at least 3' × 3' × 5'. Place the litterbox in one corner and make sure there is comfortable flooring. This should do the trick, because your cat will want to avoid fouling the small area that she is living and sleeping in.

Vacation Anxiety

Leaving your cat for extended periods of time can upset him, and nervousness might cause him to soil the house or engage in other destructive behaviors. Try not to board your cat out of the home while you are gone; this can throw cats for a loop. Opt instead for a cat sitter who your cat knows and trusts, and have this person come into your home once or twice each day to scoop litter, feed your cat, and play with him. Allowing your cat to remain in his "territory" will minimize complications and prevent the stress that results from being around numerous strangers, unknown animals, and foreign sounds.

If it isn't possible to have someone come into your home while you are gone, send kitty on a little vacation of his own, to a friend or relative's home. Again, this should be someone the cat knows and trusts. Bring the cat's own litterbox, food dishes, toys, and other familiarities, to ease the time away from home.

MARKING IN THE HOUSE

As discussed earlier in this book, both males and females mark in order to attract mates, claim their territories, ensure an adequate food supply, and reproduce.

Cats typically don't spray urine inside the very center of their territories. However, an extremely dominant male or female cat may spray if the home is large and there are many people coming and going.

Breaking the Pattern

First, of all, neuter that cat. An unneutered cat will spray in the home, especially when sensing the presence of strangers or other animals, even if they are outside! If your cat has been spraying for a long time and you finally get him neutered, he may still spray out of habit. If this is the case, try the following "aversion therapy" techniques.

1. Clean the sprayed areas thoroughly with an odor neutralizer, available at a pet shop, and treat with commercially available cat-repellent scents.

2. Spray your cat with water from a spray bottle if you catch him in the act.

3. Place double-sided sticky tape around commonly sprayed areas. Strips of aluminum foil, shallow pans of water, or sheets of crinkly newspaper also work well.

4. If these booby traps fail to stop the spraying, place small dishes of dry food near where the cat likes to spray. Cats do not like to spray near food, so this may help to break the habit. Remove the booby traps if you use this food technique.

If none of these techniques eliminate spraying, reduce your cat's territory by confining her to one room or a large wire crate for a week or two. Then slowly reintroduce her to the rest of your home, one room at a time. Minimizing territory gives the cat less reason to spray. Of course, you can avoid this ordeal by having your cat neutered before six months of age.

Cat Tales: Outdoor Cats Will Spray

Any cat allowed to roam unsupervised outside the home will spray his outside territory, even if neutered. By allowing your cat to go outside, you inadvertently encourage this habit of spraying. This is just one more reason to keep your cat inside right from the start.

Remember that even the most confident, secure cat can become an indoor sprayer if a new animal or person is suddenly introduced into the home. This is an invasion of the cat's core territory; the cat considers this a major threat, and may spray in response.

Introduce a new animal slowly, using the crating/confinement technique described in Chapter 8.

A timid or nervous cat does not need much to stress her out. Often just a quick visit from a stranger will be enough to prompt inappropriate behavior, including spraying. A nervous, unsure cat may spray as a way to comfort herself with her own scent. Fostering a safe, secure environment and helping the cat to become accustomed to strangers will help this problem.

Even remodeling your house can sometimes provoke a cat to spray as a response to the new, unfamiliar surroundings. Try to change things gradually, one room at a time, and keep things as stable as possible.

In the case of all these scenarios, follow the steps listed above, clean the areas thoroughly, neutralize odors, and use aversion techniques if necessary. However, in the case of timid cats, it's better not to use a spray bottle, as this might stress the cat out even more.

Cat Tales: Strays Encourage Spray

The regular presence of stray cats outside your home may provoke your cat to spray inside as a way of confirming her territorial status in the face of possible "invasion." This spraying usually occurs at or near doors and windows. Don't encourage cats to come around your home by feeding them, and certainly don't allow your cat outside. If your neighbor's cats are the ones roaming, ask them not to allow their cats on your property.

Fecal Marking

Though it is much less common than spraying, cats sometimes do mark with feces. Fecal marking is often precipitated by some major upset in the cat's routine. Moving into a new home, bringing another animal into the home too suddenly, or making any other abrupt change could do it. A stray who has spent much of his life outside is more likely to fecally mark in the home. Indoor-outdoor cats living in an area with many outside felines often practice this blatant marking technique as a way of dealing with severely restricted territorial options. If you have taken in a stray or your cat spends time outside, your home will be more susceptible to fecal marking.

An extremely dominant cat often does not bury his feces as a sign to other cats (or humans) that he's the "big boss" and you shouldn't mess with him. Remember, cats bury feces to hide their presence from others and to demonstrate submissiveness to a more dominant animal. If a cat feels that he is in control, he might fecally mark to underscore this point.

Unneutered males are most likely to mark fecally. Do not wait until your macho male is leaving presents in your bathtub: Neuter him early!

Beyond neutering, you can minimize the chances of your cat marking with feces by socializing him to all sorts of people and animals from an early age; getting two cats when they are kittens; keeping your felines in the home; and maintaining a stable home environment.

If need be, reduce your cat's territory and slowly reintroduce him to the rest of the home once he begins to use his litterbox reliably again, as explained previously in this chapter.

SCRATCHING

Cats in the wild scratch their claws on trees, posts, or whatever is available, to loosen old claw coverings. The behavior is, however, largely a marking behavior normally occurring at the outer boundaries of a cat's territory. Raking claws on an object leaves visual *and* scent evidence of the cat's presence—cats have scent glands in their paws. This behavior, though natural in the wild, can cause damage in the home. Fortunately, it isn't hard to change this behavior.

Generally, if your cat tends to scratch in one spot, you can be pretty sure that the behavior is one of "claw conditioning" and basic stretching. If, however, the cat scratches in numerous places, particularly at or near doors and windows, chances are your cat is marking her territory.

Appropriate Alternatives

Recognize that cats need to scratch and provide your feline with an appropriate place to scratch to her heart's content. As discussed earlier in the book, you should give your cat a few substantial scratching posts covered with sturdy rope or rug, and possibly even purchase or build a kitty "condo/playland" if you have enough space for one of these large structures. (See Chapter 5.) Place items in different areas of the home and encourage your cat to use them. Keep scratching posts near areas where your cat likes to scratch inappropriately, such as the living room sofa or draperies. Whenever you see your cat using one of the posts, praise her and give her a treat. In the case of the kitty condo, you can hide treats up in the top enclosures, or hang teaser toys off it to make it even more inviting.

You can reduce or stop improper scratching by trying any or all of the following:

1. Spray your cat with a spray bottle when you catch her scratching. Try to do this from six to eight feet away, so that the cat does not directly associate the water with you. Timing is important; the water should hit the cat just as she begins to scratch, so she will realize that the scratching is what caused the unpleasant stream of water.

2. Treat the most abused objects in the home with a commercially available cat repellent, which will smell unpleasant to the cat.

3. Place double-sided sticky tape, crumpled sheets of newspaper, or aluminum foil on the most commonly scratched areas. All of these things feel unpleasant under foot.

The Facts about Declawing

Declawing involves the surgical removal of a cat's nails (often just the front nails).

Many owners declaw their cats before they've even tried to modify bad scratching habits. Avoid declawing at all costs. For one, your cat must undergo general anesthesia, which is always a risky procedure with a small animal. Declawing is also quite traumatic for a cat. Further, you might be signing your cat's death warrant if she ever gets outside accidentally and then does not have her claws to defend herself or climb up a tree to get away from an aggressive dog.

Instead, focus on corrective training techniques to minimize scratching problems. Often it's as simple as providing your cat with a proper scratching post, encouraging her to use it, and then rewarding her when she does so.

Claw Shields

Claw shields are plastic guards that glue onto cats' nails, so they can't shred your home furnishings. These aren't easy to apply; your vet may need to attach them for you. They also need to be replaced every six to eight weeks, as old nails are shed. Most cats hate them at first but eventually learn to tolerate them. Though time-consuming, they are a valid alternative to surgery.

EATING PLANTS

Though primarily carnivores, cats do consume some vegetable matter on a regular basis. And, as most cat owners will attest, the domestic kitty likes to chew on and eat garden plants and houseplants. Although domestic house cats don't need to munch plants for vitamins and minerals (they get all their nutrition from good quality dry and canned food), they may be eating the green leafy stuff to calm their stomachs. Cats often vomit after eating vegetation, which may help to bring up undesirable substances such as hairballs. Of course, cats might also eat plants simply because they like their taste, texture, and smell. Just look at how crazy cats get over catnip!

Whatever cats' reasons, plant eating can be not only annoying but also potentially dangerous, especially if a cat is allowed outside, where toxic garden and landscaping plants grow. (See Chapter 5 for a list of toxic plants.)

Aside from never buying houseplants that are toxic to cats, such as dieffenbachia, ivy, and philodendron, here are some other ways to protect your plants from your cat and your cat from your plants:

1. If your cat goes outside (even if you supervise him), make sure you do not have any toxic shrubbery or garden plants, including azaleas, rhododendrons, yews, bean or tomato plants, or mushrooms.

2. Move indoor plants up off the floor, preferably onto pedestals or tables no wider than the base of the plant's draining dish, so that your cat has as little an area as possible to stand on while trying to munch leaves. When possible, use hanging planters.

3. Cover the soil of each plant container with marbles or rocks, to prevent your cat from digging or standing on the soil.

4. Purchase cat repellents (available in pet shops) that are safe for use directly on a plant's leaves.

5. Place double-sided sticky tape, aluminum foil, or pans of water around the area where you keep your plants.

6. Keep plants in one or two groups instead of spreading them throughout your home; this will make them easier to protect. It will also be easier to teach your cat to stay away from these one or two specific areas.

7. If you catch your cat in the act, spray her with water.

8. Make sure your cat has some grass seedlings to chew on to her heart's content. (You can grow your own at home.) Place your cat grass in an accessible area far from your houseplants, maybe near the cat's food dish, and encourage your cat to chew on that, instead of your houseplants. You can also get catnip seedlings from your local nursery. Let your cat munch on them, or dry the leaves and place them inside a sock or yarn ball.

9. Keep your cat's environment stimulating. Chewing on houseplants can be a sign of boredom, so provide your feline with lots of toys, a kitty condo, a cardboard box, or a few paper bags to hide and play in. Also, as suggested earlier, consider getting two kittens instead of one; they will amuse each other and never get bored.

BEGGING

One of the disadvantages to using too many treats to encourage new behaviors is that your cat might become a little beggar. Begging can be tiresome, especially when you are trying to eat your dinner in peace. There are several steps you can take to nip this behavior in the bud:

1. Feed your cat at regular times instead of free-feeding him.

2. Avoid giving random treats without expecting your cat to do something in return.

3. Never feed your cat from your plate, and never give him treats while you are sitting at the dinner table.

4. Avoid giving your cat "people" food—stick to cat treats.

5. Keep a water pistol on the table as a deterrent if your kitty is already a shameless little beggar. Don't use a plant spray bottle in this case—the stream of water might be too strong. Stick with a small water pistol instead—it's gentler, but you'll still get your point across.

JUMPING AND CLIMBING

Nothing is worse than a cat who jumps on the counter and sticks her whiskers into everything you're preparing for dinner, or one who insists on climbing all over a special piece of furniture, even though it's off-limits. As mentioned above, never, ever reward begging behavior, keep your cat on a regular feeding schedule, and squirt the little culprit with water when you catch her in the act. You'll also deter jumping and climbing if you avoid leaving food out on counters and tables, clean all surfaces thoroughly after you eat, and store all food out of your cat's reach. Double-sided sticky tape and aluminum foil will also aid you in this quest—these things will deter most cats from jumping and climbing on tables, counters, and furniture. You can spray smooth surfaces with a water/alcohol solution, or cat repellent. Just test these things out first to be sure they don't mar the furniture's finish.

THRILL OF THE HUNT

Much to the chagrin of many cat parents, centuries of domestication have not done away with the cat's love for hunting. Most of us don't want our cats to decimate the fauna surrounding our houses. Pets get all the food they need at home, and prey animals such as rats, bats, and squirrels can carry infectious diseases, including rabies. And besides, who wants to find little corpses all over the place? Once again, don't allow your cat to roam outdoors freely. Also remember that even if you let your cat outside into a contained area such as the back yard or on your balcony, the swift little hunter can still do plenty of damage. Attaching a few small bells to your cat's collar will make it harder for her to sneak up on birds or other small animals, but bells aren't foolproof. Keep a close watch on your kitty!

AGGRESSION

Aggression is a part of every animal's life at some time or another. As upsetting and unwanted as aggression might be, there are times when it is natural and justifiable: Just think about a mother cat protecting her young from attack or a cat who snaps at tormenting children. On the other hand, aggression in cats can also be abnormal, as is the case with aggression that is genetically based, rooted in fear, or triggered by overly dominant tendencies.

Whether "normal" or "abnormal," aggression in cats can be upsetting and dangerous to an owner who does not understand it or is not prepared for it. Reacting incorrectly can intensify the behavior rather than reduce it. Aggression is the most common problem behavior next to house soiling, and so understanding the different types of aggression and their causes will make you a much better cat owner. If your cat shows profoundly aggressive tendencies toward you, other people, or other animals, see your vet or a feline behaviorist ASAP.

Hereditary Aggression

Just as cats can be born with extra toes, they can also be born with a predisposition toward aggression. This problem is difficult to predict; the parents' behavior is often the only tip-off. Fortunately, this type of aggression is quite rare, and, in the case of purebred cats, it's usually prevented easily through judicious breeding techniques. A good breeder would never allow aggressive male or female adult cats to breed, even if they were perfect physical specimens.

A cat who has a hereditary predisposition toward aggression may give no discernible warning of the coming behavior. However, these kittens often show deviant behavior when quite young; instead of playing and romping with littermates, they may be perceptibly antisocial from the time they're only three or four weeks old. Fortunately, you'll probably never experience this problem with a cat, unless you fall prey to an unscrupulous breeder or adopt a mixed breed from faulty bloodlines.

Avoid dishonest or amateur breeders—stick with professionals who have impeccable reputations. In the case of mixed-breed cats, observe the mother, if possible, as well as the rest of the litter. Watch for any signs of unpredictable, aggressive behavior, or anything out of the ordinary, such as one kitten's desire to be alone or attack the other kittens without justification.

Fear-Based Aggression

When cats find themselves in threatening situations, the "fight or flight" instinct can really kick in. Fear aggression in a cat can be directed toward animals or humans. Fear is also relative: A confident Siamese might consider a certain interaction fun, while a reserved Persian might perceive the same thing as an unwanted, scary intrusion. If your cat is playful, outgoing, and gregarious by nature, chances are he will not often show fear aggression toward you or other persons. However, if your cat is naturally timid and reserved, she may become easily daunted by strangers who try to pet her or pick her up. If such a cat feels threatened enough, she could bite or scratch a well-meaning person. Fear aggression stems from many causes. Feline parents who are nervous and timid tend to pass those personality traits to their kittens; these easily stressed kittens are more likely to be afraid of strangers and unknown circumstances, and to show fear aggression.

Remember that improper socialization at an early age plays a big part in the likelihood of antisocial behavior. Also, cats have incredible memories and they don't forget past trauma—this can lead to aggression as well.

When cats demonstrate fear-based aggression, their body language makes it evident. Their ears go flat against their head, tails lash back and forth, pupils dilate, they hiss, their hair stands on end, and often they strike out with their front paws. Some fearful cats, when feeling that there is no possible escape route, will simply go belly-up and brandish all four paws in the air, ready to fight an attacker if necessary.

Cat Tales: No Hitting

Never hit your cat, no matter what he's done, unless you are defending yourself or another. Hitting your cat will destroy the trust you have both developed, and your cat will probably be wary of you for the rest of his life. Hitting always compounds existing problems; there are other more effective ways to improve behavior.

There are things you can do to help prevent fear aggression or at least minimize it. First of all, refer to earlier chapters in this book and choose your kitten carefully from a reputable source. Observe her behavior before you take her home and make sure that she knows how to socialize properly and that she appears to be friendly and outgoing around people and other animals.

Remember to socialize your cat as much and as soon as possible! Teach your kitten to walk on a leash, make her home as stimulating and fun as possible, and slowly try to desensitize her to unusual sounds and behaviors. Instruct children and adult guests never to chase after a cat for any reason. Instead, let new people feed your cat treats and offer him toys. This will endear guests to the cat and quell any fearful reactions. Also make sure your timid cat's litterbox is located in an area that isn't subject to heavy traffic, especially from strangers. A timid cat who suddenly finds herself cornered in a small bathroom with a person she fears can flip out and attack out of desperation. In general, if you create a safe, secure environment for your cat, it will help a lot with fear aggression.

Territorial Aggression

By now, you've learned that cats are very territorial. In the wild, cats space themselves out so as not to intrude on a neighboring cat's "turf." This voluntary spacing helps to prevent conflicts and ensures that all will have adequate access to prey.

Domestic cats have the same territorial instincts. The quest to protect perceived territory varies from cat to cat, depending on gender and level of dominance. Though females can demonstrate territoriality too, it's more common in males. In the case of male cats, competition for mates often results in aggression in the wild; this is also the case with unneutered domestic indoor-outdoor cats.

But even if yours is a strictly indoor cat, he still may exhibit signs of territorial aggression. (Neutering your cat before six months will help to curb the tendency.)

The home is a cat's territory, and most cats—even outgoing, gregarious ones—will show some initial concern when a strange person, cat, or dog comes into the home, no matter how friendly. Remember, your cat accepts you and your family (other, familiar animals included) unconditionally because all of you are his foster parents and siblings; strangers are a totally different story. A territorially aggressive cat will hiss at, chase, and attack other strange cats (and sometimes people) who come into his territory. His ears will be pointed, his tail will lash back and forth, and his hair will stand on end.

As is the case with fear aggression, you can minimize territorial aggression.

Avoid choosing an overly dominant, pushy little fur ball; also steer clear of one who seems to guard and hoard food or toys obsessively. As always, observe the mother's behavior (just don't confuse natural maternal protection with aggression), and make sure the kitten has been socialized properly.

When choosing an adult cat, carefully observe his reaction to your presence. Is he protective of toys and food? Does he have any fresh scars or wounds from fights with other cats?

Remember to introduce new animals into the resident cat's world very slowly, and use the crate/confinement method if necessary. And don't forget that it's always best to raise two kittens or a puppy and a kitten together from a very young age.

If your cat has been neutered but still shows a high level of territorial aggression, you may need to separate him from other pets entirely. Also see your vet to discuss possible drug therapies.

Maternal Aggression

If you ever adopt a pregnant stray, be forewarned that a feline mother with newborn kittens can be a vengeful spitfire. Most mammalian mothers protect their offspring quite fiercely, and female domestic cats generally have the same protective instincts. Although some cats make terrible mothers and abandon their litters (which then have to be bottle-fed), most are great mothers, and take their jobs quite seriously. They will normally prohibit outsider contact with their kittens until they feel the time is right. Trusted owners can usually handle the kittens after the first week or two with the mother in the room.

The good news is that maternal aggression never lasts long; normally the behavior subsides after a few weeks.

Play Aggression

As you've already learned earlier in this book, through play with their littermates, kittens learn to stalk and attack prey, and hone their timing, coordination, and stealth. Some cats never grow up, and continue to demonstrate this stalking "play" aggression with their human families. These cats are not being truly aggressive, fearful, or territorial, they're just being overly assertive with you. And even though they don't mean any harm, when this type of rough play leads to biting and scratching, it can be a problem.

Cat Tales: Duration of Your Deterrent

In the case of all deterrents suggested in this chapter, it's important that you use them for at least six weeks in order to effectively change your cat's behavior.

Cats who get carried away with this type of play aggression are just being immature and restless. Often, they're solitary indoor cats who are bored with being alone all day and want some fun when you come home. Once again, you can fix this problem fairly easily by neutering your cat, providing her with as much stimulation as possible at home, and by bringing home two kittens instead of only one, so kitty doesn't get lonely.

Be ready to correct the aggressive attacking behavior when it occurs. Learn to anticipate the times when your cat is most likely to play-attack, and have your water spray bottle ready. Or, clap your hands together loudly while saying "No!" You can pick up a kitten by the scruff when you say "No!" Just don't shake the kitten, as you could hurt him. And don't try this with adult cats—they might scratch you.

Competitive Aggression

As with all animals, competition between cats for anything desirable can often cause conflicts. A choice toy, a treat, or even a pat on the head can prompt aggression. Rivalries between two cats of equal stature can cause a game of play stalking to erupt into an aggressive outburst.

In the home, cats will normally work out their dominance hierarchy among themselves. Dominant and submissive cats quickly learn their places, and the submissive cat backs off when the dominant one really wants something. When two cats are very close in stature, however, aggression can occur over competition for some plaything or your attention.

Beyond neutering your cats, you can also discourage competitive aggression between cats by doing the following:

1. Avoid having too many cats in a given space. Normally, two cats are all you should try to manage in an apartment or small home. If you have more than that, you risk reducing each cat's territory below comfort level. Overlapping territory can cause fiercer competition.

2. Let your cats work out their dominance hierarchy on their own, and stay out of conflicts unless the cats really lay into each other.

3. Provide the cats with plenty of toys and distractions, and have at least two of everything, including food dishes, scratching posts, and litterboxes, to avoid squabbling.

4. Encourage each cat to sleep in a separate area if they are extremely competitive with each other.

5. Feed each in a different area, and give the dominant cat her food first.

6. Give individual time to both cats; they each need to feel wanted and loved by you. Completely ignoring one in favor of another will increase the chances of competitive aggression.

7. Separate the cats if the competitive aggression becomes too intense.

Redirected Aggression

Have you ever struggled to get through a hard day at work, only to come home and quickly lose your temper with your spouse or children for no good reason? That's redirected aggression. All emotional beings experience these frustrating, seemingly unjust outbursts at one time or another.

Cats are no exception. After being stressed by an injury or some other nerve-wracking experience, cats sometimes lash out at their owners. For instance, the afternoon right after a veterinarian visit is prime time for a cat to exhibit redirected aggression.

Usually, victims of redirected aggression are trying to be democratic and helpful. But because they just happen to be at the wrong place at the wrong time, they end up taking a beating. If you sense your cat may be ripe for this sort of aggression, avoid close physical contact with him for a while after he's had a traumatic experience. Don't try to pick him up—he might bite or scratch. Let the cat calm down on his own, and wait for him to come to you.

Beyond following all of the usual recommendations suggested elsewhere in this chapter, the best thing you can do is keep your cool. If your cat shows redirected aggression, remember it's not a deliberate reaction, and punishing the cat will only reinforce the behavior.

Sickness or Injury-Induced Aggression

This is another form of redirected aggression. Pain can cause cats to vent their frustrations in the same way they would right after returning from a visit to the veterinarian. A cat who shows hostility due to sickness, injury, or any other sort of pain is just responding to internal rather than external stimuli.

Whether a child pulls a cat's tail or a cat injures himself, pain will cause a cat to become stressed and irritable. In this state, cats are likely to unleash their anger on the nearest victim, namely you. Serious medical problems such as bladder or kidney infections, epilepsy, parasitic infestations, arthritis, or tumorous growths can also cause pain and ensuing aggression.

Preventive health care is always important, but if and when your cat does become sick or injured, first take the appropriate steps to get her back on her feet. Follow your vet's instructions, and make the cat as comfortable and secure as possible. Consider confining her to one room while she's recovering, to prevent her from hurting herself and to minimize any upsetting stimuli that might provoke aggression. Leave the cat alone if she seems irritable or stressed, and don't let other people or animals pester her.

Biting the Hand That Feeds You

There are times when some cats who are otherwise enjoying petting and stroking from their owners unpredictably lash out to scratch or bite. They seem to suddenly reach a saturation point regarding handling, and, rather than simply leaving the premises, they exhibit "corrective" aggression. It's as if they're saying, "That's enough petting right now, though I may want you to pet me again in a second or two, so I'll just stay here in your lap." If your cat shows this type of aggression, limit petting and grooming sessions to just a minute or so, and always stop before the cat becomes stressed or irritated. Watch for body language cues; if you see the tail lashing back and forth, or the ears going back and the body tensing, end the session and get away from the cat.

Also put the cat on a regular feeding schedule instead of free-feeding, then periodically give her treats, especially as a reward after a handling session.

If your cat is particularly timid or unpredictable, don't initiate physical contact—wait for the cat to come to you by rubbing against you, for instance.

Cat Tales: When to Seek Behavioral Help

Sometimes, cats' behavior problems can stem from something as straightforward as an improper diet; other times, the cause can be more complicated, such as improper socialization. If after implementing the suggestions in this chapter your cat still exhibits problem behaviors, consult your vet and a qualified feline behaviorist. They may need to play detective for a while before discovering a solution to your cat's problem.

Kitty Health Care
and First Aid

You can help to prevent many disorders from seriously affecting your cat simply by taking precautions, and by being properly prepared for sickness or injury if and when they do occur. As a cat parent, you have a responsibility to provide your cat with the most supportive and safe environment possible. You also need to know what to do if your cat hurts himself and what physical symptoms call for a trip to the vet ASAP. This chapter will discuss ways to safeguard your cat's health, including basic first-aid techniques, and in-home care that could forestall serious illness complications in case of emergencies.

CHOOSING A VETERINARIAN

Choosing a veterinarian for your kitty is an important decision, and the choice should be made before your cat has a problem or you need a vet's services in a pinch. There are several things you should look for when deciding on a veterinarian.

Location and hours of operation: You should be able to find a capable vet within ten or fifteen minutes of your home. Make sure the hours are convenient; it helps if the office is open late at least a few days a week, so you can take your kitty in for visits after work.

Emergency care: Emergencies can arise at any hour of the day or night. Be sure your vet either provides round-the-clock emergency care or is able to refer you to a nearby emergency clinic.

Reasonable prices: For most devoted pet parents, money is no object when it comes to the well-being of their beloved animals. Nevertheless, health care costs really add up. Be mindful of prices, but don't let this be your only criterion. Also, beware of high-volume vet clinics that seem too cheap to be true. They could be cutting corners somehow.

Good organization: A vet's office should be clean, well organized, and professional, and staff should be efficient and polite. Avoid vet clinics that seem chaotic, rude, and disorganized.

Strong communication: A good vet is easy to talk to, willing to listen, and as good with people as she is with animals. Avoid a vet who seems rushed, impolite, or put off by questions. Choose someone who seems knowledgeable, kind, and genuinely interested in the health of your pet. If you don't feel at ease, move on.

Participation: With the exception of surgeries, taking radiographs (x-rays), or emergency procedures, a vet should always allow you to be present during your pet's examination.

Knowledge: Stick with a vet who keeps up with the most current medical information and tries to improve his skills through continuing education and training. Beware of vets who "swear by the old ways." A full-service clinic that is able to perform all procedures on premises, plus refer you to specialists if need be, is ideal.

You should take your new kitten or cat to the veterinarian within a week after she comes home. This initial visit will determine your cat's general state of health, ensure that she has no infectious diseases, give her the proper vaccinations, and begin a good vet/pet relationship. Be sure to bring a fecal sample!

How to Find the Right Vet

There are four basic ways to find a good animal doctor. You can, of course, simply look in the yellow pages for the vets nearest to your home, but you won't know anything about them or their reputation this way. Asking friends or relatives for vet suggestions is a better method. If someone you know has stuck with their vet for years, that's a good sign. Also, the shelter from which you adopted your cat can probably recommend a few reputable vets in your area. Shelters deal with hundreds of animals and often have sick ones in need of medical attention, so they know good doctors. Likewise, if you purchased your cat from breeders near your home, they can recommend a good vet in your area, possibly their own.

ANNUAL CHECKUPS

Make sure to take your cat in for a checkup at least once each year. During these annual checkups, your vet will give your feline a thorough physical exam, which should include:

- Examining the cat's body, from nose to tail. The vet will search for lumps, growths, swelling, skin or hair abnormalities, parasites, or abscesses.

- Weighing the cat and checking her temperature.

- Listening to the cat's heart and lungs.

- Checking the cat for abnormal discharges from any bodily orifices, including eyes and nose.

- Determining the condition of the cat's teeth, gums, and ears, as well as the scent of the cat's breath (often a sign of sickness).

- Palpating (or feeling) the cat's internal organs to check for infection.

- Testing the cat's skin elasticity to determine if she is dehydrated.

Your vet may also take a fecal sample from the cat (often requested beforehand, at the time that you call to make the appointment), to determine if your cat has a parasitic infestation. If you schedule a visit because of a suspected illness, your vet may also take blood and urine samples for testing.

During this visit, your vet will also administer any necessary vaccinations or booster shots. Kittens receive their first vaccinations at about eight to ten weeks of age, followed by boosters about one month later, and then again at one year. Although after-one-year boosters used to be given annually for the rest of a cat's life, new recommendations from the Association of American Feline Practitioners suggest subsequent boosters be given at three-year intervals. The rabies vaccine is slightly different; kittens first receive it at about three months of age, they're boosted at one year, and then subsequent boosters are repeated at three-year intervals. In general, you need to customize your cat's vaccine schedule based on age, exposure to other cats, and whether she stays strictly indoors or goes outside sometimes.

PREVENTING PARASITIC INFECTIONS

Cats and kittens can acquire internal parasites from contact with infected stool, food, or water; from nursing; or from fleas. Cats can also contract internal parasites by consuming infected prey, such as mice. Contact with the feces of another animal spreads a variety of pests, as does drinking infected water. Cats who have access to the outdoors are likely to pick up one or more of these pests sometime in their lives, due to many of these causes. This is yet another reason not to let your cat roam outside.

If you live in an area of the country that gets warm and humid much of the year, your cat will run some risk of acquiring heartworm, though it is much more common in dogs. Talk to your vet about this; he might decide to prescribe a monthly heartworm pill.

Cat Tales: A Safe, Clean Environment

Ensuring that a cat's home environment is safe, secure, and clean is one of the easiest ways to prevent illness and reduce the chance of infection. Keep the home clean to avoid infectious germs; steer clear of toxic plants, chemicals, and dangerous substances; maintain a clean litterbox; and regularly wash food and water dishes to minimize bacterial buildup. Also, keep your kitty away from any aggressive animals—even if they are family and friends' pets.

External parasites, such as fleas and ticks, are common during the warmer months. Even indoor cats can suffer from external parasites, though. Remember, these parasites have the ability to hitch rides into your home on the backs of other animals, or even on you. To prevent fleas and ticks, you should:

1. Consider using a flea-and-tick collar on your cat (just not on kittens—they can be toxic to young animals). (Always be sure to use products approved for cats.)

2. Inspect your cat daily for any external parasites. During times of bad infestation, consider using a vet-approved topical flea-and-tick powder or spray (again, these are not for kittens). If you find even one flea on your cat, give her a flea bath, using a vet-approved flea shampoo.

3. Discuss using bombs, sprays, or powders with your vet. When applied properly to carpets, furniture, and drapery, they can eliminate these pests from your home, as long as you treat your cat at the same time. (Be careful: Children, pregnant women, the elderly, and those with respiratory problems may react adversely to these products.) Newer once-a-month topical treatments are also now approved for cats.

HANDLING WITH CARE

You probably play with, handle, and cuddle your kitty quite a lot, so why not use that handling time as an opportunity to do a quick physical exam? Here are things to look for:

A lustrous coat: A dry coat falling out in patches can indicate a dietary deficiency, allergic dermatitis, dehydration, parasites, or fungal infection.

Clear, slightly pinkish skin: Dry, flaky skin can point to allergies, parasites, or dehydration; crusty, ulcerated skin can indicate dermatitis, parasites, indolent ulcers, or dietary deficiency.

Lumps or swelling: Either might reflect the beginning of a cancerous growth or a sign of trauma. A swollen abdomen could point to gastritis or worm infestation, and a constantly full bladder might indicate a urethral blockage due to stones. Swollen lymph glands around the neck could mean infection or cancer as well.

Bad breath: Unpleasant mouth odor could indicate gastritis, cancer, kidney problems, or diabetes.

Healthy teeth and gums: If gums are pale or white, that could indicate anemia or other serious conditions. While looking in your cat's mouth, examine his teeth and gums for signs of plaque or tartar, often the harbingers of periodontal disease.

Healthy legs, feet, and tail: These should be free moving, with no pain whatsoever. Move each leg within its full range of motion; this can help you detect injury or an arthritic condition. A kinked tail could point to fractured vertebrae in that area.

Healthy footpads and nails: These should be free of foreign objects, cuts, and bruises. A thorn stuck in a pad can cause great pain, lameness, and infection. Overgrown nails can affect the cat's posture, damage furniture, and injure you.

Healthy reproductive organs: A cat's penis or vulva and anal area should be free of any discharge; these could point to a kidney or bladder infection, pyometra, worms, infected anal glands, or other serious infections.

You can do all of these checks in a short time, and they need not be traumatic to your cat. After performing this daily once over, give your cat a great treat, and soon he won't mind these "exams" so much.

KEEPING AN EYE ON ELIMINATION HABITS

Any drastic changes in your cat's elimination habits can indicate an ongoing or upcoming health problem. Be watchful, so you can spot sudden breaks in habits and act as necessary. What should you look for?

Change in frequency: Any time a cat suddenly begins to urinate or defecate more or less frequently than is normal *for her*, you should be on your guard for some health problem. Diarrhea, constipation, or unpredictable urination can be symptoms of a variety of conditions, including diabetes; food poisoning; gastritis; kidney or liver problems; allergies;

intestinal blockages; kidney or bladder stones; urethritis; parasitic, viral, or bacterial infections; cancer; or dietary deficiency. A cat who runs to the litterbox frequently without passing any urine or only tiny amounts of urine may have urinary blockage, which can be life threatening.

Pain during elimination: If the act of elimination causes your cat any pain, it could point to stones, infection, poor diet, or other problems. Meowing forlornly or rocking from side to side during elimination are both signs of distress and discomfort, and should be investigated by a vet.

Amount of waste: A dramatic increase or decrease in urination could be indicative of a bladder or kidney infection, diabetes, a blocked urethra, or some type of serious infection that is causing your cat to dehydrate. Variation in the volume of feces passed can point to infection, intestinal blockages, cancer, gastritis, food poisoning, or other problems.

Condition of stool: Normal stool should be fairly firm and dark brown. If your cat's stool has suddenly become loose or black in color (indicative of bleeding in the stomach or small intestine), there could be a problem. Blood on the stool means hemorrhoids or bleeding in the large intestine; you might see worms in the stool if your cat has a parasitic infection. Tapeworm segments are usually noted; roundworms are not.

Color of urine: If your cat's urine appears to be dark, deep yellow instead of paler yellowish-green, it may indicate dehydration or the passing of an abnormal amount of urea, indicative of a kidney problem. Clear urine may point to excessive thirst or provide a clue that your cat is feverish or developing diabetes or another disorder.

Odor: Pay attention to abnormal smells. Extremely malodorous stool can point to a bad diet or the presence of some toxic condition. Unpleasant-smelling urine can mean diabetes or improper diet.

Location of eliminations: Avoiding the litterbox is typically a behavior problem (see Chapter 9), but it can point to health issues. When a cat is feeling poorly, she often wants to be alone and may seek out isolated areas to recuperate. Or, if a cat's waste is offensive to her (in the case of worms or serious infection, for instance), she may not want to "pollute" her litterbox. These things can lead her to eliminate in odd locations.

Always see your vet right away if you notice these or any changes that concern you.

KEEPING YOUR CAT ACTIVE

Cats need exercise just as much as humans do. While cats might not fetch as avidly as fido, they certainly love to move around, and they need to work their muscles, heart, and lungs. Some cat breeds are naturally more active than others. In fact, people who have Abyssinian or Siamese cats probably wish they could slow their little wildcats down! If you have a more sedate, reserved breed, such as a Persian or Himalayan, you might have a hard time getting your cat off the couch.

Cat Tales: Quiet Time

Just as activity is important to keep your cat fit and alert, so is rest a key part of a healthy life for any animal. Well-rested cats tend to be happier, healthier, and more relaxed than those who are sleep-deprived. Cats, especially kittens, need a lot of sleep, usually over fourteen hours each day, to keep fit and mentally alert, and to prevent illness and stress. As long as your feline isn't taking a catnap in a dangerous spot, do not disturb!

Whatever the case, obesity in a cat is not physically or mentally healthy. Make sure your cat gets enough exercise—it burns calories and allows your cat to let off steam. Play ball or throw toys for your cat to chase (this usually appeals to a cat's natural prey instinct) and encourage her to walk on a leash from an early age.

And tricks aren't just for dogs. Beyond "come," cats can learn to do all sorts of tricks, including how to spin, jump, play ball, fetch, roll over, and much more. The key is positively reinforcing your cat with praise *and* treat rewards each time she obeys a command or performs a trick correctly. Finally, remember the benefits of getting two kittens instead of one. Lifelong companions, they will chase each other and play together throughout their adulthood. This will help them to remain physically active and psychologically and emotionally healthy as well.

GIVING YOUR CAT MEDICINE

Cats aren't always the easiest patients when it comes time to give them medicine. Have no fear; with practice, it's not so hard. Here is one good way to give your cat a pill:

1. Hold the pill between the thumb and forefinger of one hand.

2. Place your other hand atop the cat's head; position the thumb and forefinger of this hand at the corners of the cat's mouth, hooking them into the mouth slightly.

3. Tilt your cat's head back until the nose points straight up, so her mouth will open.

4. Quickly place the pill onto the back-center portion of your cat's tongue.

5. Close her mouth and hold it for a few seconds while massaging the cat's throat, to ensure she swallowed the pill. At this point, it also helps to blow into your cat's nose: This startles cats, which then prompts them to swallow.

If your cat really gives you trouble swallowing pills, some medications can also be crushed and then mixed into canned cat food. You might try compounding as well, which involves having medications made up into treats or flavored liquids.

WATCHING FOR RED FLAGS

In addition to the aforementioned symptoms of impending illness, there are other specifics you should pay attention to and report to your vet. These include:

- A temperature of 103 to 105 degrees Fahrenheit.

- Diarrhea or vomiting in combination with a fever or other signs of illness.

- Severe dehydration, which you can diagnose by lifting and releasing a pinch of skin on the cat's back. If it takes more than a moment to rebound, your cat may be dehydrated.

- Persistent lethargy combined with poor appetite and weight loss.

- Bad breath combined with excessive thirst.

- A cough or wheeze accompanied by fever.

- Runny nose or eyes, with a cough or fever.

- Persistent limping or obvious pain in the limbs or spinal column.

- Any lumps or swollen areas that seem painful and warm, or those that are discharging pus or blood.

- Pale gums and lethargy, possibly combined with loss of appetite or fever.

- Failure to pass urine, as urinary blockage can be life threatening.

If your cat displays any of the following symptoms, take a trip to the vet immediately:

- A fever of over 105 degrees Fahrenheit.

- A fever of over 103 degrees Fahrenheit accompanied by severe shortness of breath, extreme lethargy, and lack of appetite.

- Complete or partial paralysis.

- Signs of possible toxic substance consumption, including difficulty breathing, excessive lethargy, vomiting, or diarrhea.

- Any wound that won't stop bleeding.

- An infected abscess accompanied by persistent high fever.

- Serious trauma from an attack by another animal or person.

- Cessation of breathing or loss of consciousness.

- Broken limbs or trauma to the eye.

- Persistent bloody diarrhea or vomit.

Cat Tales: Good Record Keeping

Keep a medical journal that records vaccination information and any sicknesses or traumas your cat has suffered, their duration, treatment, and date of occurrence. Include what medications were used, along with their effectiveness and side effects, if any. These records can help you and your vet to determine patterns of illness, chronic conditions, or allergic reactions.

Sometimes, signs of illness can be subtle, so be aware of reduced appetite, intermittent signs of lameness, sudden changes in sleeping patterns, excessive (or nonexistent) self-grooming, excessive vocalization, or increased irritability. You are the best judge of your cat's moods, habits, and general state of mind. If you are picking up on subtle changes, trust your gut feelings, and, when in doubt, see your vet.

TAKING KITTY'S TEMPERATURE

Most cats don't like having their temperature taken, but it is often an important part of diagnosing what is wrong with your kitty.

Clean a rectal thermometer with soap and water, rinse it well, and then shake it down to below 98 degrees Fahrenheit. Apply petroleum jelly to the tip, and also put some on the cat's anus. While a trusty friend stands the cat on a table, lift her tail and insert the thermometer with a straight push, about an inch or so. Be careful not to put sideways pressure on the shaft, which could break the tip. Leave it in for at least one minute. If kitty's temperature is between 101 to 102.5 degrees Fahrenheit, she's fine.

Cat Tales: Kitty First-Aid

As noted in Chapter 5, you should have a well-stocked first-aid kit handy to deal with emergencies as well as minor situations that don't necessarily require a visit to the vet. If you already have a first-aid kit put together for your family that should do just fine, though you may want to add some extra gauze rolls and adhesive tape. Keep the first-aid supplies in a small container, and store it in a convenient, accessible location.

CARING FOR CUTS AND SCRAPES

You can effectively treat some minor skin injuries at home. However, deep wounds, wounds that have severed an artery and will not stop bleeding, serious burns, breaks in the skin caused by a compound fracture, and animal bites all need the quick attention of a vet, though you can perform preliminary treatment on these injuries in the interim.

For scrapes that barely break the skin (these sometimes occur on the cat's foot pads) clean the affected area with anti-infective solution, then treat with antibiotic ointment (ask your vet or pharmacist for recommendations). Try to distract your cat for a few minutes after putting ointment on a scrape, so the ointment can soak in and your cat doesn't immediately lick it away.

A bandage might not be necessary; just be sure to clean the scrape twice each day until it begins to heal and the threat of infection has passed. Reapply the antibiotic ointment each time you clean the wound. If any signs of infection appear, see your vet.

Most cuts in the skin stop bleeding fairly quickly. Deep cuts or those that continue to bleed for more than five straight minutes require veterinary attention. In the interim you can minimize bleeding by applying direct pressure to the wound with a gauze pad.

Secure the gauze pad by wrapping rolled gauze around it. A short period of direct pressure will often quell the flow of blood and allow clotting to begin.

When the wound is on the tail or a limb, wrap from the wound down to the end of the appendage; this will prevent swelling and minimize oxygen debt to the parts below the wound. If the wound is on a part of the cat's body you cannot wrap, apply direct pressure with a gauze pad for ten minutes and see if the bleeding stops.

Cat Tales: Bubbles Spell Trouble

Carefully observe any wounds on your cat's chest, to ensure that there are no air bubbles in them—an indication of a punctured lung. This serious condition requires immediate veterinary attention. Surgery may be needed to correct the problem.

Keep It Covered

Some wounds should remain covered for a few days. Wrap leg and tail wounds with roll gauze followed with adhesive tape (the wrap should not be as snug as the pressure bandage). Change this bandage at least once per day, or whenever your cat chews it off, which *will* happen. If it's a back or stomach wound, wrap a large white cloth around the cat's middle, tie it either on top or bottom, then secure it with adhesive tape. Protect a neck wound with a handkerchief tied bandanna-style. A vet should always check any wound that requires a bandage.

BANDAGING FRACTURES OR BREAKS

Sprains or muscle pulls will not normally call for bandaging or splinting, but you may need to confine your cat to a crate or small room for a few days to limit movement. In case of a serious leg fracture or break, if the lower portion of the leg is dangling freely, you will need to stabilize it immediately with a splint. Find a heavy piece of cardboard or another appropriate stiff object. While a friend holds the cat, wrap the injured leg carefully with cotton padding; a disposable diaper will work well. Secure this lightly with adhesive tape, then tape the splint to the padding. Make sure to cover any exposed fractures with gauze and tape to limit infection. Then go to the vet, ASAP!

APPLYING TOURNIQUETS

When serious wounds don't respond to a pressure bandage, you may need to use a tourniquet, a last-ditch technique while preparing to go to the vet clinic. Never a first choice, tourniquets can, if applied improperly, cut off all blood flow to areas below the wound, effectively starving those tissues of vital oxygen. Tissue death can result; in severe cases, the affected limb or tail may need to be amputated.

Cat Tales: Taking a Pulse

The easiest place to feel a cat's pulse is on the inner surface of one of the rear legs, right where it meets the body. A large femoral artery passes close to the surface here; you should find it quickly. Count the pulses for fifteen seconds, then multiply by four to get the correct beats per minute.

Use a length of rope, surgical tubing, or cloth, form a loop or slip knot, and tighten it around an area a few inches above the wound. *Do not overtighten;* only increase pressure to get the bleeding to slow to a trickle. Release the tourniquet every ten minutes to allow oxygen to flow to tissues below the wound. After twenty or thirty minutes, try using only a pressure bandage. Someone should be driving you to the nearest emergency clinic while this is happening.

CAR ACCIDENTS

In the event your cat ever sneaks out of the house unsupervised and is unfortunately hit by a car, the situation could be very serious. *Do not panic.* Remember, your cat will need your help more than ever if he does become seriously injured; stay cool and put on your thinking cap. Here's what to do:

Assess your cat's injuries immediately. Is he conscious or unconscious? Bleeding or not? Do you see evidence of broken bones? These important assessments are crucial to treatment. Remember, a cat can have extensive internal damage even if there are few external signs.

Stay with the cat, and call out for help. The car's driver or some other bystander can make a cell phone call for help. If the driver took off (barbarian!) and there is no one in sight, yell your head off until someone notices you.

Keep the cat still. Do not move a seriously injured cat unless absolutely necessary. Movement could exacerbate potential spinal cord damage. If the cat is moving around, be prepared to immobilize him by holding him if necessary. Your cat might be panicked, so you could take some serious licks, including bites and scratches, but this is a small price to pay for ensuring your cat's safety. Gloves, a blanket, or a towel work well here for human protection. Do not let the cat run away, whatever you do. Gingerly placing the cat in a travel crate is the best way to keep him calm and still; place a blanket inside the crate to comfort the cat and keep him warm.

Carry the cat carefully and slowly. If you absolutely must move the cat, nestle his head in the crux of your elbow, with his body resting on the inside of your forearm. With your free hand, hold the cat firmly by the nape of his neck, to prevent him from leaping out of your arms.

WHAT IF A CAT GOES INTO SHOCK?

An animal is said to be in shock when her tissues are not being adequately supplied with blood and oxygen. Most often caused by a severe drop in blood pressure due to blood loss (internal or external bleeding), shock can easily kill a cat if not treated quickly. Telltale signs include:

- Weak, rapid heartbeat that gets fainter over time. Often the pulse will be imperceptible, even though the heart is still beating.

- Falling body temperature. The cat's extremities may feel very cool to the touch.

- Very pale or white gums, indicating failing blood circulation. If the gums are white, it means the brain is also being starved of oxygen.

- Disorientation, lethargy, and unresponsiveness to any stimuli. The cat may seem "out of it," and could lapse into a coma.

Any cat showing signs of shock needs to see a vet as soon as possible; delay could prove fatal. In the interim, keep the cat as warm as possible.

ANIMAL ATTACKS

Your cat could be seriously hurt or killed if attacked by another animal, whether by direct trauma or by the transmittal of infectious diseases such as rabies. If your cat is ever attacked by another animal (including a human), immediately take her to the vet, in case she has sustained serious cuts and tears, or broken/fractured bones. Up-to-date vaccinations will provide crucial protection for a cat if ever attacked by another animal; *do not be lax on these.*

If your cat sustains a puncture wound from an animal bite, clean and dress it properly. Punctures can easily abscess; they should be irrigated well with antibacterial solution and kept as clean as possible to prevent infection. Antibiotics might be necessary. Serious cuts, tears, scratches, or punctures may require suturing.

After an animal attack, check your cat's mouth for broken or missing teeth. Broken teeth require veterinarian treatment.

Snake and Insect Bites

Though rare (few cats hunt these creatures), the occasional unlucky cat does get bitten by a rattlesnake, water moccasin, gila monster, or other venomous reptile. If you witness the attack or get there right away, apply a tourniquet several inches above the affected area (unless it is on the face or body). Get to the vet *pronto.*

Although insect bites and stings can be painful and may cause swelling, they are rarely fatal, unless many bees, wasps, or hornets sting a cat at once, or a cat has a severe and unusual allergic reaction. Only black widow spiders and scorpions are capable of killing nonallergic cats with their venom.

If your cat is stung, quickly remove stingers and clean the affected area thoroughly. Repeatedly apply a cool cloth to minimize swelling and pain. If you see symptoms such as vomiting, disorientation, or shock, see your vet as soon as possible.

BURNS

Though rarely fatal, a serious burn is very painful, and it can lead to infection. In extreme cases, shock and death can occur. *Do not* put butter or any ointment on burns without checking with your veterinarian first!

Chemical burns occur if a cat gets into extremely acidic or alkaline materials, such as pool chemicals, car battery acid, drain cleaners, or furniture strippers. The burned area may or may not appear blistered or bubbled. Often, hair will fall out, and skin may discolor. Flush an external chemical burn with large amounts of cool water, cover it lightly with a bandage, and then get to your vet right away.

Electrical burns often occur when a cat chews on a power cord. These burns appear most often on their mouth and head area. The surface burns are of secondary importance to the shock. Keep the cat immobile and warm, and get to the vet. A cat who has suffered a serious electrical shock may stop breathing, or might go into cardiac arrest. If this occurs, you will need to perform artificial respiration/cardiopulmonary resuscitation (CPR) while on your way to the vet. If the cat seems okay apart from the external burns, treat the area with cold water and cool cloths, cover it with a light bandage, and go to the vet.

Cat Tales: Getting Shots

There are several common vaccinations your cat may need. Rabies is required by law every three years, but the other vaccinations listed here should be customized for your individual cat and her lifestyle. These include feline panleukopenia (distemper); feline leukemia; feline infectious peritonitis; feline viral rhinotracheitis, chlamydia psittaci, and feline calicivirus (all respiratory diseases). Giardia and ringworm are other possible vaccinations.

Heat burns from a car engine, steam iron, or a fallen pot of boiling water can be extremely painful and damaging to the cat's skin and coat. Apply cold water and compresses immediately, bandage lightly, and make a trip to the vet. Serious burns invite systemic infection and require extended care, including frequent dressing changes and antibiotic therapy.

POISONING

If your cat has ingested a poisonous plant or another toxic substance, you may need to act quickly to save his life. The most common treatment is inducing vomiting, to remove the toxin from the cat's stomach before it gets into the system. However, never induce vomiting if a cat has ingested a corrosive material such as drain cleaner, acid, chlorine powder, tarnish remover, fertilizer, or fuel of any type. Forcing these harsh substances back up will further damage the cat's esophagus and oral cavity.

To induce vomiting, administer two teaspoons of hydrogen peroxide. Although in the past, syrup of ipecac was sometimes recommended for this purpose, the ASPCA's Poison Control Center does not recommend this for cats. If hydrogen peroxide is not available, use two teaspoons of heavily salted water (you may need to repeat this second option). After the cat has vomited, give her as much fresh water as you can; force-feed with a turkey baster if need be. Then get to your vet as soon as possible. Do not attempt to induce vomiting if the cat is losing consciousness or is having seizures.

Other techniques for minimizing the effects of poison can be used, including activated charcoal tablets, which can absorb many poisons and prevent their absorption into the cat's system.

You can call the **ASPCA's Animal Poison Control Center,** twenty-four hours a day, for advice. Their telephone number is **1-888-426-4435**. Your local 911 service might also be able to give you advice. However, it's best to have the telephone number of an emergency cat clinic on hand for times like these.

Of course, prevention is always the best course of action. Keep all toxic substances out of your cat's reach!

CHOKING

Though rare, choking can occur if a large piece of food or some other object becomes firmly lodged in a cat's throat. If your cat is unconscious, you will need to perform artificial respiration and perhaps CPR as well. If the cat is still conscious, remove the obstruction with your fingers, forceps, or tweezers. If you can't reach the object, lay the cat on his side, place the heel of your hand below the last rib (where the diaphragm is), and give two or three quick pushes, straight down. This feline version of the Heimlich maneuver should force air up the windpipe and dislodge the object. Get your cat to the vet as soon as possible. Ideally, you should be performing first-aid on your cat in the car while someone else drives you to the clinic.

HYPO- AND HYPERTHERMIA

Hypothermia, a condition resulting in profoundly reduced body temperature, occurs rarely in cats. However, cats who have lived all their lives indoors, if suddenly subjected to outdoor winter conditions, can become seriously cold to the point of mortal danger. Even cats used to cool outdoor temperatures, when subjected to subzero conditions, can suffer hypothermia. Kittens left out in the cold are perhaps the most threatened. Symptoms of hypothermia include reduced body temperature; disorientation and lethargy; uncontrollable shivering; decreased respiration and heart rates; and possible frostbite. Never let your cat outside on a frigid winter day!

In mild cases, simply bringing the cat indoors and wrapping him in a blanket should help to get his body temperature back up to normal. Use a heating pad or hot-water bottle to speed up the process. Do not leave a cat unattended on a heating pad, however. More serious cases may call for immersing the cat into a bath of about 105 degrees for a short period, then drying him with a towel and hair dryer and wrapping him in a blanket. Any cat who does not respond quickly should be taken to the emergency clinic.

Cat Tales: Temperature Regulation

Cats become more sensitive to temperature fluctuations as they age, especially when it comes to cold winter weather. Staying warm becomes crucial, so keep your cat inside, and out of damp, chilly situations.

Hyperthermia is the opposite condition, when a cat becomes overheated from extreme temperatures. It is often caused by poor ventilation combined with hot weather. The perfect example is an animal left in a car on a hot summer day with all the windows closed. A cat accustomed to cool temperatures can also suffer hyperthermia if suddenly moved to a very hot climate.

Hyperthermia can kill a cat quickly. Symptoms include high body temperature; disorientation and dehydration; vomiting; accelerated heart rate and respiration; and panting. Get an overheated cat into a tub of cool, even tepid, but not cold, water as soon as possible, or hose him down. After the kitty has cooled off, see your vet to ensure that no permanent damage has been done.

You can prevent hyperthermia by providing your cat with plenty of fresh clean water. Never leave a cat in a hot car, especially with the windows rolled up, and never leave him in a travel crate in a hot stuffy area for too long. Keep your home at a comfortable temperature, and wet your cat's coat down on horrendously hot days. Many cats also enjoy laying by a fan on hot days.

SEIZURES

Identified by sudden uncontrolled muscle movements, seizures can be caused by a number of factors, including poisoning, injury, and epilepsy. Some cats, according to the cause, might have only one seizure at a time, spaced out over days or even weeks, whereas others can suffer multiple seizures in a very short period.

A cat in a convulsive seizure can be a great danger to herself and to you. The cat may not even recognize you, and so may bite or scratch you—or anyone who tries to restrain her. If you can predict when the seizure is about to occur, the best course of action is either to wrap the cat in a blanket or place her in a small travel crate to restrict movement and prevent injury. Seizures require medical treatment.

PERFORMING CPR

A person or animal needs CPR in cases of no pulse or heartbeat, unconsciousness, or cessation of breathing. CPR should begin no longer than a few minutes after heart or breathing functions cease, or else permanent brain damage and death can result.

If your cat has stopped breathing:

1. Place him on his side, open his mouth, pull the tongue out, and check for any foreign objects that might be stuck.

2. Check for mucus or blood buildup, then close the cat's mouth and place your mouth over his muzzle, completely covering the nose.

3. Blow gently into his nose and watch to see the cat's chest expanding. Repeat this twelve times per minute for as long as necessary.

4. If there is no pulse or heartbeat, combine cardiac compression with artificial respiration. In between each breath (given every five seconds), place the middle three fingers of your favored hand over the cat's heart, at about the fifth rib; press with medium pressure, then release. The ribs should compress in about one inch. Compress the chest five times in between breaths.

5. Continue compressions and artificial respiration until you get to the vet, or until the cat begins breathing on his own again.

MAINTAINING THE HEALTH OF AN OLDER CAT

Cats, like humans, are living longer these days, and a healthy, well-cared-for cat can live upward of twenty years, aging almost imperceptibly. Most cats slow down so gradually that we hardly notice.

If you pay close attention, though, you'll see the telltale signs. An older cat may begin to put on some weight as her metabolism slows (though often this is balanced by a waning appetite). The cat's coat may become slightly less dense and may dry out and flake more easily. The cat's senses also become less acute over time, but again, it happens so gradually that it is hard for you or the cat to notice until late into the cat's life. (Fortunately, touch sensitivity remains fairly constant, perhaps right to the end; cats may even rely on touch more in old age due to the failing of other senses.)

The cat's internal workings change with age as well. Bones become more porous and brittle, increasing the chance of a break or fracture. Flexibility decreases, and joints become stiffer and susceptible to arthritis. Reaction times also slow, and memory capacity is somewhat reduced also. The cat's immune system and general resistance to infectious disease decreases.

Some feline disorders particular to the aging cat include:

- Cancerous tumors, especially among unneutered cats.

- Loss of appetite; try adding some odorous foods (such as sardines or fish oil) to the meal.

- Thyroid disease: hyperthyroidism is common, but hypothyroidism is very unusual in cats.

- Electrolyte deficiency, or a lack of potassium due to kidney and liver failure, which can cause weight loss, lethargy, and anemia. Supplementation with potassium pills can often cause marked improvements.

- Diabetes, caused by reduced pancreatic function.

- Arthritis, or inflammation from wear and tear on the joints, which causes pain and restricts movement. Older cats with arthritis may not be able to groom themselves well and will need your help.

- Constipation, stemming from the decreasing stomach and intestine efficiency and failing colon activity. The addition of fiber to the diet, as well as a vet-approved laxative, can help.

- Cataracts, the substantial clouding of the lenses of the eyes. Cataracts can obscure vision, but surgery can help.

Cat Tales: Think Twice about New Company

Avoid getting a new, frisky, active pet if you have a senior cat at home. In his desire to play, the younger cat will annoy the older cat, which could lead to overexertion or stress for the older feline. Let your old pal live out his golden years in peace, free from competitive tension.

Common Illnesses and Health Problems

F rom colds to cataracts, and tumors to tapeworms, the domestic feline can contract many illnesses. Most will develop minor problems at some point in their lives, and a smaller number will suffer some major ones that require substantial veterinary care. This chapter is your handy A to Z guide to feline ailments, their causes, and treatments. Most of these conditions are either preventable or treatable if handled properly.

ABSCESSES

An abscess is a pus-filled cavity in the skin that harbors high levels of bacteria. Usually the result of a bite or a scratch, if left untreated, it can spread infection throughout the body. Toxin buildup in the blood can lead to fever and sometimes death. A cat who is neutered early and kept indoors will rarely suffer from abscesses, unless he gets into fights with another indoor pet.

If you handle and groom your cats regularly, you'll discover an abscess, not only from the discharge and swelling but also from the cat's behavior. The cat will be in pain and may isolate himself, meow constantly, or lick the wound excessively.

Your vet may need to open the abscess up slightly with a scalpel and flush it with an antibiotic solution, then suture it or put in a drain. You also might need to give your cat additional antibiotics and apply warm compresses to increase blood supply to the area and speed up healing.

ALLERGIES

Caused by an exaggerated response of the immune system, allergic symptoms occur only after the second contact with the offending allergenic material has been made; the first exposure simply sensitizes the body. The immune system mistakenly identifies relatively harmless substances such as pollen or a specific type of food as foreign invaders, and antibodies and lymphocytes attack these benign agents. During the process, different chemicals such as histamines are released, triggering allergy symptoms.

Exposure to certain chemicals, dust, pollen, or food can all trigger allergies. Cats can develop allergies to many different substances. Be it fleas, food, medicine, shampoo, or a parasite allergy, cats can become disoriented, upset, and miserable. Itchy skin, labored breathing, hair loss, watery eyes and nose, and severe diarrhea and vomiting are all possible effects. Some allergies are difficult to diagnose, and your vet might need to perform extensive blood and skin tests to determine the offending material. Stress can also cause allergic-type reactions in a cat.

Treatment can involve avoiding the offending substance, and drugs such as antihistamines, which relieve itching and congestion, can also be used. Steroid-based drugs (topical cream or pill) can help prevent symptoms as well.

You can do your best to prevent allergic reactions in your cat by feeding the best food possible; keeping stress levels down; avoiding potentially toxic shampoos, conditioners, or flea powders; and keeping your cat indoors and your home flea-free.

ANEMIA

Relatively uncommon in cats, anemia involves a reduction in the number of red blood cells in the body. These cells, which contain hemoglobin, supply oxygen to the rest of the cells in the body. Internal bleeding, decreased production of red cells by the bone marrow, dietary deficiencies, or infection can all cause anemia. If allowed to continue without treatment, it can be fatal.

Signs of anemia include decreased appetite, body weight, and activity; pale or white gums (instead of pink); incontinence and diarrhea; and increased respiration. Your vet can accurately diagnose anemia with a blood test. Treatment will vary according to cause; transfusions, vitamin and mineral supplements, or anticancer drugs are all possible options. You can prevent diet-induced anemia by feeding your cat a diet your vet has approved. You can also prevent injury-induced anemia by keeping your cat out of fights with other animals and ensuring that she doesn't fall from a great height, which could cause internal bleeding.

ARTHRITIS

A painful disease of the skeletal joints, arthritis is characterized by swelling, stiffness, and inflammation. Affecting one joint or many, symptoms vary from mild discomfort to severe pain and deformity.

Osteoarthritis is degenerative. Cartilage covering the ends of each bone begins to wear away with age. Since cartilage acts as a lubricator, its absence causes discomfort, swelling, and abnormal bone growth. Normally a disease of the aging cat, osteoarthritis can occur in younger cats with birth defects or those who have suffered joint injury.

Rheumatoid arthritis, rare in a cat, involves more pain and swelling. With this disorder, the cat's immune system actually attacks and damages joints and surrounding tissues, often resulting in deformity. (Cats can also develop hip dysplasia, which will be discussed later in this chapter.)

Signs of arthritis are numerous. Your cat will seem slower and not as agile. She may often be temporarily lame after exerting herself, as well as extremely sensitive to touch in and around the affected areas. In advanced stages, the cat may not be able to get around at all.

Your vet may take X-rays of the affected joints to examine the extent of damage. Joint fluid can also be drawn and examined to determine if infection is present. Blood tests can reveal the presence of proteins typical with rheumatoid arthritis.

Though not presently curable, arthritis can be treated. Anti-inflammatory or antibiotic drugs (for arthritis triggered by a bacterial infection of the joints) can be used.

Cat Tales: Steer Clear of Acetaminophen

Never give your cat acetaminophen (Tylenol) or ibuprofen-based drugs—they are lethal to cats. Although it's usually not a wise idea to give cats aspirin, it is sometimes used, but only under careful veterinary supervision. Aspirin can routinely help dogs and humans, but even low dosages can be fatal to a cat.

You can help to prevent or ease arthritis in your cat by making sure she's not overweight; giving her a warm, soft, dry place to sleep; giving her some exercise, which helps to keep joints mobile; using a heating pad under the cat's bed when necessary (make sure it's not too hot, and supervise); and seeing an animal chiropractor if necessary.

ASTHMA

Asthma affects the respiratory system and causes great difficulty breathing. Recurrent, unpredictable attacks of breathlessness, accompanied by wheezing, can vary in severity. Though uncommon in cats, if a cat does have asthma, it often begins at a young age and then either disappears or worsens as the animal ages.

Untreated bronchitis, along with inhaled infectious, irritating, or allergenic agents can bring on asthma. In older cats, cardiac asthma can be brought on by a failing heart and subsequent fluid retention in the lungs, making breathing and oxygen transfer difficult.

During a bad attack, the cat's breathing can become very labored, heart rate can soar, and the animal can become panicky. A severe attack can be fatal.

Your vet can diagnose asthma through a variety of tests, including X-rays, blood tests, and examination. Although not presently curable or completely preventable, asthma attacks can be minimized. If an allergen is the cause, that substance should be totally avoided. An asthmatic cat who reacts badly to pollens should be kept indoors with the windows closed. Keeping the level of dust down in the home, using an indoor air filter, reducing stress, and eliminating cigarette smoke can help.

Your vet can prescribe certain drugs to help alleviate the condition, including steroid-based injections or pills that help to open up bronchial tubes.

Any bad asthma attack requires a trip to the emergency clinic, where the staff will administer oxygen and bronchial dilators to get the cat breathing again.

BRONCHITIS

Bronchitis is defined as any inflammation of the bronchial tubes, or airways in the lungs. Respiratory infection brought on by a cold or the flu, an inhaled irritant, or an allergy to food, dust, pollen, cigarette smoke, medications, or other substances can cause it. Bronchitis is more common among older cats, but can occur at any age. Symptoms include coughing, gasping, sneezing or wheezing, fever, loss of appetite, or sluggishness.

Acute bronchitis can come on quickly and clear up just as fast. Often caused by viral infections, this type of bronchitis is more common in the winter months, especially in cats allowed outdoors. The cat will have a persistent cough that produces yellowish or green sputum. A low-grade fever may also be present.

Chronic bronchitis has similar symptoms but lasts much longer, often for months. The strain put on the respiratory system can cause permanent injury. In chronic bronchitis, the bronchial walls become thicker over time, reducing the volume of the airways and consequently the amount of oxygen that can enter the body. Injured passageways also become more susceptible to infections, which then cause further damage.

When left untreated, bronchitis can progress into asthma, emphysema, or bronchial pneumonia, all serious conditions that can threaten a cat's life. Any cat recovering from bronchitis should be kept warm and sedentary. An expectorant can be administered to help bring up mucus and fluid collecting in the bronchial passages. Antibiotics are also often prescribed for any infection present. A vaporizer can help, too. High exertion should be avoided for several weeks, even after the cat has seemingly recovered.

CANCER

Cancer is abnormal growth of tissue in the body that spreads unchecked. Malignant cancer tumors most commonly form in major organs such as the stomach, lungs, breasts, intestines, skin, liver, or pancreas. Cancers can, however, develop anywhere in a cat's body, including bone marrow, muscles, or lymph glands. A common cause of death in old cats, cancer can be both painful and difficult to cure.

Unlike benign growths, such as warts, which tend to stop growing at a certain point, malignancies continue to grow and infiltrate surrounding tissues. Also, cancerous cells can break away from one growth, spread to other areas via the blood vessels and lymph system, and *metastasize*, forming new malignant tumors independent of the original.

Cancers are common in cats, and can occur at any age. Growths can remain undetected for long periods of time, especially in the thoracic (chest) cavity, where their size remains hidden. Cancer can have many origins; possibilities include diet, environment, radiation exposure, genetic predisposition, and even viruses sometimes (think feline leukemia).

The range of symptoms is vast, depending on the type of cancer and stage of development. Look for appetite or weight loss; decreased activity; increased irritability; difficulty breathing; blood in the urine; persistent coughing; diarrhea or incontinence; blotchy or bumpy growths on or under the skin that seem to get larger; bad breath; wounds that fester and do not heal; any abnormal discharge from the eyes, ears, mouth, anus, or reproductive organs.

A veterinarian diagnoses cancer by examining the cat and tissue cells obtained through biopsy. X-ray or ultrasound tests or an internal exam using an endoscope can also be used to diagnose cancer. Tests on blood, urine, and stool samples can also be used.

Treatment includes drug therapy, surgery, chemotherapy, radiation, diet change, or a combination of any or all. Many cancers are completely curable, and survival rates continue to climb. However, cancer can often be fatal in cats, so waste no time having it treated.

Prevention is difficult, as it is so often caused in part by hereditary factors. A well-balanced diet combined with regular exercise can help reduce the chance of occurrence, however.

CATARACTS

As your cat ages, you may notice that the lenses of his eyes slowly take on a bluish-gray tint; this is part of the aging process, brought on by the gradual increase in tissue density and the decrease in lens fluid level. Cataracts normally do not cause pain or greatly interfere with a cat's vision and may not require treatment.

If the lens becomes opaque, however, the cat's vision will be impaired, night vision will be dramatically decreased, and nearsightedness can also result. Lens opacity is commonly caused by old age, but eye trauma from a fight or a projectile can also cause it. Cataracts can be associated with severe diabetes or the ingestion of certain toxic chemicals. Treatment usually involves surgery, which can reduce or remove the opacity of the lens and improve vision.

Protect your cat from corrosive chemicals, and keep him indoors and away from other combative cats who could injure his eye. A proper diet is also essential, because it can prevent diabetes and obesity, two conditions thought to contribute to cataract formation.

COCCIDIA

Protozoan parasites that can infect a cat's intestinal tract, coccidia often occur in kittens and young cats raised in less-than-clean surroundings. Once infected, your kitty can develop diarrhea and become weak, dehydrated, and underweight. Though uncommon, these parasites can infect a cat, dog, or you.

One particularly obnoxious coccidium, known as *Toxoplasma gondii*, can cause intestinal problems, plus tissue damage and long-lasting illness. When a pregnant woman contracts this organism through contact with wastes in her cat's litterbox, she runs the slight risk of her unborn child developing birth defects in utero. Though the odds are rare, doctors recommend that a pregnant woman avoid cleaning her cat's litterbox during pregnancy.

Diagnosis usually involves bringing in a fecal sample for your vet to examine. A number of oral drugs kill off these parasites.

To prevent you or your cat from being infected with *Toxoplasma*, keep her indoors; cats usually acquire this protozoan through killing and eating mice and birds. If your cat is always inside, you will not have to worry about this problem. Also avoid feeding your cat raw meat. Finally, resist bringing a stray cat into your home unless you first take him to the vet to have him checked out.

CONJUNCTIVITIS

An infectious inflammation of the inner eyelid, conjunctivitis is a common ailment in cats and humans alike. Often seen as a symptom of various respiratory infections, it can, if left untreated, cause permanent eye damage.

Symptoms include excessive tearing, discharge from the affected eye, squinting, or keeping the eye closed. This discharge can go from clear to a thicker yellow, evidence of increasing bacteria. In more severe cases, the conjunctiva (the lining of the inner lids and white of the eye) can become pinkish-red and swollen, which is why this disease is often commonly referred to as "pink eye."

Newborn kittens often have conjunctivitis. Caused by bacteria in the mother's uterus, this condition must be treated by your vet, to prevent permanent eye damage. Treatment normally involves antibiotics. The cat's eyes must also be kept as clean as possible.

Though preventing conjunctivitis in newborn kittens is impossible, you can reduce occurrence in adults by maintaining a clean environment and keeping your cat indoors.

CONSTIPATION

In most cases constipation (trouble passing feces) is a temporary and harmless condition that can occur in cats of any age. Occasionally, it can point to other more serious disorders, particularly in older cats. Most cats will defecate at least once per day, although regularity is more important than frequency. Whenever a cat's normal habits of defecation suddenly change drastically, it could be a sign of illness or disease.

Other than the obvious lack of defecation, symptoms are loss of appetite, irritability, restlessness, or vomiting. In serious cases the cat may become lethargic and bloated, and may run a slight fever. Causes can include old age; lack of fiber in the diet; weakness in abdominal muscles; reduced intestinal motility or liver function; hypothyroidism; general lack of activity; cancer, especially of the colon; stress; excessive hair ingestion or some other type of intestinal blockage; spinal injury; and dehydration.

First visit your vet to rule out serious causes. He or she will then discuss at-home remedies that might help alleviate the problem. You can increase the fiber content of your cat's diet by feeding her mostly dry food that has been soaked in water. You can also add fiber supplements to your cat's food. One-quarter teaspoon of olive oil once a day will help to move things along, too.

Increasing your cat's level of activity can stimulate bowel action, and regularly brushing and combing will minimize hair ingestion. Lastly, have plenty of fresh, clean water available for your feline. If the water in the cat's dish is not changed daily, the cat may eschew it and become dehydrated. A dehydrated cat will have very hard stools that will be difficult to pass.

CYSTITIS

An inflammation of the bladder lining, cystitis, common in older cats, is normally caused by high levels of bacteria. This condition can result if the cat has had any type of obstruction preventing her from urinating regularly and completely. Stagnant urine in the cat's bladder or urethra can provide the perfect environment for these microorganisms to grow.

Stones or tumors can cause blockages leading to urine retention and infection, as can a structural blockage, particularly the narrowing or collapse of the urethra itself. Kidney damage or disease can also cause cystitis.

Symptoms are varied and include frequent need to urinate, with only a small amount of urine passed; pain during urination, usually indicated by meowing or crying; odorous urine; irritability and restlessness; unexplained aggression; and fever.

Your vet can diagnose cystitis by examining a urine sample. Excess bacteria are the main indicator; your vet may grow a culture to confirm the type of bacteria. Small amounts of blood might also be present in the urine.

Treatment often involves putting the cat on antibiotics to clear up the infection, which normally takes a few days. In rare situations, surgery may be needed to repair a collapsed urethra or remove a blockage. If the cystitis is a symptom of a more serious condition such as cancer, or liver or kidney failure, the treatment of those conditions takes precedence. True urinary blockage is a serious emergency that can lead to death if not treated.

Make sure to give your kitty ample amounts of fresh, clean water each day; regular water intake will help to flush out the bladder and prevent bacteria buildup. Scoop your cat's litterbox each day and change litter regularly. If litter is dirty and foul smelling, your cat may avoid it and hold back urination, which leads to cystitis. Lastly, make sure that your cat gets plenty of exercise to keep all systems functioning happily.

DEAFNESS

Defined as the partial or total inability to hear, deafness can result from congenital defects. It can also be caused by disease, injury, or old age.

Conductive deafness is caused by the faulty transportation of sound from the outer to the inner ear, often due to damage to the eardrum or the three bones of the middle ear (the malleus, the incus, and the stapes). Sensorineural deafness is caused by failure of sounds to be transmitted from the inner ear to the brain due to inner damage to the ear or the acoustic nerve, which connects the inner ear to the brain.

Possible causes of conductive hearing loss are ear wax buildup; middle ear infections that cause excess fluid buildup or tissue damage; loss of stapes bone motility; and damage to the eardrum from infection, injury, or surgery. Possible causes of sensorineural hearing loss include congenital defects of the inner ear; damage to the cat's inner ear from sickness or injury; prolonged exposure to loud noises; old age; viral infections; and tumorous growths on the acoustic nerve.

Gradual hearing loss occurs more frequently in cats than it does in dogs. Any older cat with a hearing deficiency should not be allowed outside, especially near busy roads; he will not hear danger coming and could get hurt or killed.

Deafness from birth is uncommon in cats but does occur, particularly in cats who carry the genes for a white coat, and more so if they also have blue eyes. White, a color rarely occurring in the wild, has been overencouraged in domestic breeding programs, and this has resulted in physiological problems. Choose a breeder wisely.

Create a safe, quiet environment free of potential trauma and infectious agents. Keep your cat's ears clean, and see the vet at least once a year. Most cats can easily adapt to being deaf, provided they are kept indoors in a predictable environment.

DEHYDRATION

Dehydration can occur when an animal's output or expenditure of water exceeds its intake. During dehydration, the body also loses essential minerals, including salt.

When a cat becomes ill, the thirst drive can become inhibited, leading to dehydration. Fever, bacterial or viral infections, or injury can all cause a cat to stop drinking (and eating).

Certain illnesses can cause a cat's body to lose water, including diarrhea or vomiting, diabetes, kidney disease, fever, or overheating.

Symptoms can include severe thirst; increased heart rate and respiration; dry mucous membranes in the mouth, eyes, and nose; decreased skin elasticity; decreased circulatory system efficiency; and disorientation, owing in part to low blood pressure.

Providing water and treating any accompanying illnesses will work to correct dehydration in most cases. In more serious cases, your vet may need to administer fluids to the cat, either subcutaneously (under the skin) or intravenously (in a vein). These fluids contain water and salt to restore proper electrolyte balance.

To prevent dehydration, give your cat plenty of fresh, clean water daily; keep the temperature of your home comfortable; and make sure your cat is healthy and receives proper checkups.

DENTAL PROBLEMS

Maintaining healthy teeth and gums is important to your cat's well-being; without strong teeth, eating is difficult and discomfort is frequent.

Common dental problems include plaque, which leads to tartar formation; cavities; lost or broken teeth; gingivitis (gum) and periodontal disease; and oral cancer.

To reduce plaque and calculus (hardened tartar), feed your cat a primarily dry-food diet. Also inspect your cat's teeth regularly and clean them at least once or twice a month with a cotton swab dipped in warm water and baking soda. You can also use one of the toothpastes made especially for pets—these come in flavors such as poultry. Once calculus has formed, only your vet, using an ultrasonic tool, can remove it. The cat must undergo general anesthesia for this.

Cavities, though relatively rare in cats, can occur, particularly if excessive plaque buildup is present. If you suspect that your cat has a cavity, see your vet, who can successfully treat it and perhaps save the tooth.

Lost or broken teeth cause havoc in a cat's mouth. Infections and abscesses can occur, causing gum problems, pain, and possibly additional tooth loss. If your cat loses or breaks a tooth, see a vet immediately. When plaque and tartar build up around the base of the teeth, the bacterial toxins produced cause the gums to become swollen, inflamed, and tender—gingivitis. Symptoms include reddish-purple gum color instead of the healthy pink. Gums may bleed easily, especially after the cat eats, cleans itself, or chews on a toy.

Gingivitis, if left untreated, can develop into periodontal disease, an inflammation of the membranes around the base of the teeth and erosion of the bone holding the teeth in the jaw. Avoiding plaque buildup and treating gingivitis early can prevent this serious condition.

Side effects of gingivitis and periodontal disease include bad breath; loss of appetite and weight; pain, possible irritability, and aggression.

DERMATITIS

Inflammation of the skin, dermatitis is often due to an allergy but sometimes occurs without any known cause. It can cause rashes, itchiness, dandruff, and sometimes infection and sickness.

All three types of dermatitis are annoying to the cat, and can bring on irritability and aggressive behavior.

Allergic Dermatitis

When a cat is allergic to a certain substance, for example a type of food or shampoo, he can develop adverse skin reactions. Skin can become red, blistery, bumpy, and itchy, causing the cat to bite and scratch himself incessantly, to the point of creating open sores that can become infected. Affected skin will seem warm to the touch, and may become callused and thick from continued damage. Hair may fall out in patches, and skin can become infected, possibly oozing bacteria-laden pus and blood. A cat with allergic dermatitis might also have other symptoms such as coughing, sneezing, wheezing, or discharge from the eyes or nose. Treatment involves identifying the allergen and completely avoiding it if possible; prescribing antihistamines and oral or topical antibiotics; bathing with a medicated shampoo to relieve itching and combat infection; and visiting the vet regularly.

Contact Dermatitis

Any cat can have skin problems if exposed to highly irritating substances such as strong chemicals, insecticides, soaps, solvents, or paints. The symptoms are often identical to those of allergic dermatitis, but occur in specific areas rather than all over the body. For instance, many cats develop contact dermatitis from wearing flea collars, which contain strong insecticides. Treatment for contact dermatitis involves removing the offending substance as well as eliminating any other potentially irritating substances from the cat's environment. See your vet for a thorough diagnosis; some substances that cause contact dermatitis can also be toxic or fatal if swallowed.

Parasitic Dermatitis

A cat infested with fleas, ticks, lice, or mites can develop symptoms of dermatitis because these pests cause the animal to scratch incessantly. Some, particularly fleas, can also cause true allergic reactions. Many cats are allergic to fleas; even the bite from one of these little vampires can cause miserable itching and scratching. Fleas can also transmit worms, cause anemia, and spread serious disease.

Check your cat's coat and skin regularly for ticks and fleas, and also pay attention to the cat's behavior. Excessive itching, biting, and scratching; hair loss and irritability; and red rashes, bumps, and open sores are all symptoms. Treatment includes visiting your vet; limiting your cat's access to the outdoors and to other animals; keeping your home free of parasites; using one of the new once-a-month flea products that are now approved for use in cats; and treating your cat with a veterinarian-approved flea shampoo when signs of parasites appear.

DIABETES

This life-threatening disease is caused when the pancreas fails to produce the hormone insulin, necessary for the metabolism of glucose. Diabetes often occurs in older or obese cats, and it could have a hereditary component. Glucose levels in the blood skyrocket when a cat has diabetes. This can possibly cause excessive urination, thirst, and hunger; weight loss and fatigue; degeneration of blood vessels and nerve cells; dehydration and diarrhea; blindness and kidney damage; ulcerated skin; and, in extreme instances, coma and death.

To diagnose this disease, your vet will take urine and blood samples from your cat and examine them for excess glucose levels. Treatment involves administering insulin to restore glucose metabolism. Sometimes, if the cat's pancreas is still producing some insulin, special dietary regimens and oral hypoglycemic agents will suffice to keep blood sugar levels stable.

Your vet will recommend a lower-calorie, higher-fiber diet, and the cat's meals will need to be spaced out through the day to maintain a more stable glucose level in the blood. You'll need to monitor your cat's weight closely.

Diabetes is not a disease to be taken lightly; left untreated, it will certainly lead to your cat's death. If you observe any of the aforementioned symptoms, play it safe and see your vet right away. A simple blood or urine test could save your friend a lot of suffering.

DIARRHEA

Almost every cat experiences more fluid, frequent bowel movements at some time or another. Diarrhea usually results from eating or drinking food or water that is either contaminated or else simply not agreeable to that cat's system. Diarrhea in kittens is much more serious than in adults because it can quickly cause severe dehydration, often fatal in baby animals.

Causes include food poisoning; viral or bacterial infection; allergy; diabetes, liver, or pancreatic disease; cancer; inflammatory bowel disease (IBD); panleukopenia; parasites; and stress.

Treatment varies according to the diagnosed cause. See your vet, especially with a kitten or elderly cat, if symptoms do not subside within twenty-four hours. The vet will first check for any serious, life-threatening problems such as cancer or diabetes. Depending on how severely dehydrated your cat is, fluids may have to be given intravenously or subcutaneously. Urine, blood, and fecal samples will be analyzed to determine if there is a viral, bacterial, or parasitic infection. If so, appropriate medications will be prescribed. If the cause is due to an allergy, you and your vet will need to deduce what substance is causing the diarrhea. It might be a particular food ingredient such as wheat, rice, preservatives, or a certain type of meat. Once the allergen is identified, simple avoidance will usually cure the problem.

Diarrhea can also be caused by stress brought on by sudden changes in the cat's environment, including a change of food or litter; relocation to a new house; loud noises; mistreatment by humans; or the sudden introduction of another person or animal into the home. Keep your cat's environment clean and parasite-free; feed her a vet-approved food; avoid feeding her human foods; and reduce stress as much as possible.

EPILEPSY

Evidenced by recurrent seizures that cause loss of muscle and limb control, as well as profound behavioral changes, epilepsy is usually symptomatic of a larger problem. Epileptic seizures can occur as a result of head injury, brain infections, tumors, stroke, or a metabolic imbalance, such as severe dietary insufficiency or toxicity from an insect bite.

Seizures are caused by abnormal electrical activity in the brain. Normally regulated and orderly, this activity becomes chaotic and unpredictable during a seizure. Diagnosis is not simple. The veterinarian must examine the attacks and also the cat's general health, diet, and behavior. After completing a full exam (including neurological testing), a vet may decide to administer anticonvulsant drugs, change the cat's diet, or, in rare cases, perform surgery.

Some cats will outgrow the condition; for others, it will worsen, and in a few, it will stay the same. If your cat suffers from epilepsy, consult your vet, who will try to minimize the frequency and severity of seizures.

A cat who is having a seizure can be dangerous to herself and to you. After the seizure, the afflicted cat usually acts as if nothing serious happened at all, and doesn't seem to remember having been aggressive. Let the seizure run its course, and make sure that the cat's immediate environment is free of danger. You can help minimize the chances of epilepsy by reducing the cat's risk of injury or infection and keeping her indoors; assuring proper nutrition and adequate exercise; and making sure that all toxic substances are safely stored away.

FELINE IMMUNODEFICIENCY VIRUS

A retrovirus is similar in structure to HIV (human immunodeficiency virus). The virus (which affects only cats) invades the victim's body and tricks the affected cells into producing more viruses. Although it can cause sickness immediately upon infection, it often remains hidden in the host for years without causing major signs of illness. FIV (like HIV) attacks cells of the immune system, particularly certain white blood cells, known as T-cells, that serve an important role in combating infection. By weakening the cat's immune system, FIV opens the cat up to many illnesses that his body's defenses would normally deal with successfully.

FIV is transmitted from cat to cat through sharing of bodily fluids, including saliva and blood. It is thought that bite wounds are the most common form of transmission. Pregnant felines can also transmit the disease to their unborn or nursing kittens.

Cats with FIV eventually begin to show signs of infection, including fever and diarrhea; swollen lymph nodes; low white blood cell count; lethargy and weight loss; behavioral changes; seizures; skin sores that will not heal; and severe stomatitis (inflammation of the oral cavity). As the virus weakens the cat's immune system, other symptoms can appear, including secondary viral or bacterial infections, parasites, and cancers. Respiratory problems, urinary maladies, conjunctivitis, nervous system disorders, and mental deterioration are common as well.

Treatment for this lethal condition can extend the length and quality of a cat's life but will not save it. Although until very recently there was no vaccination against FIV, a new vaccine is soon to be available, as of the writing of this book. You and your vet will attempt to prevent secondary infections from taking hold, once the cat's immune system is incapable of doing so, through the use of antibiotics, special foods, vitamin supplements, and fluids (when necessary), and by making the cat as comfortable as possible. Because it is so infectious, cats with FIV must be kept indoors, away from other cats.

Preventing FIV in your cat can be as simple as keeping her indoors, away from strange cats. Choose breeders carefully, and avoid pet shops. Take your new kitten to the vet the first week you have her, so the vet can determine health status and check for FIV.

FELINE INFECTIOUS ANEMIA

Feline infectious anemia is caused by a microorganism that parasitizes red blood cells. When the cat's immune system spots these burdened red cells, it attacks and destroys them, assuming they are invaders. This eventually leads to a dearth of red cells; the cat's bone marrow cannot replace them fast enough, so there is a net loss and anemia results.

Feline Infectious Anemia spreads from cat to cat by the exchange of fluids, possibly by parasite bites, or in utero. There is now an effective treatment for this condition, but it may need to be repeated, as it is difficult to get rid of the organism (Hemobartonella) totally. Prevent it by keeping your kitty indoors, keeping strays away, and avoiding boarding your cat out.

FELINE INFECTIOUS PERITONITIS (FIP)

Another immune-defeating viral condition, FIP also has no cure and is fatal, but there is a vaccination. Caused by a coronavirus, FIP attacks white blood cells and other tissues, causing a breakdown in the body's disease-fighting capabilities. FIP is common among cats living under crowded conditions (such as a cattery or large kitten mill), and occurs most frequently among pet-shop cats.

FIP is transmitted from cat to cat through contact with urine, feces, saliva, and mucus, and can remain intact on a cat's food or water dish, or in the litterbox. Symptoms include high, intermittent fever that remains unresponsive to drugs; weight loss due to poor appetite, vomiting, and diarrhea; anemia; lethargy and depression; fluid in the lungs or abdominal cavity; kidney, pancreas, or liver failure; diabetes; disorientation and dizziness; secondary infections; and skin granulomas.

Your vet will examine blood, urine, and abdominal or chest fluids, and perform a complete physical exam to diagnose FIP. Although fatal, treatment of secondary infections can prolong life and ease discomfort.

Prevent FIP by keeping your cat indoors and away from strays. And remember, never take in a stray until your vet has checked him out and given him a clean bill of health.

FELINE LEUKEMIA (FELV)

The retrovirus responsible for this increasingly common and almost always lethal condition is transmitted through various secretions, particularly saliva. Feline leukemia causes cancer, but it also can kill an animal within days. A cat can be infected with FeLV through a bite, through sharing a litterbox or dish with an infected cat, or even by being bitten by a flea that might have previously bitten an infected cat. Mothers can infect their young either in utero or during nursing.

Like other retroviruses, FeLV tricks the victim's cells into making copies of it, bringing about cancers of the lymph nodes, blood, abdomen, and chest, along with other serious conditions. Symptoms include weight loss and poor appetite; fever; anemia; diarrhea, incontinence and vomiting; liver, spleen, or kidney failure; seizures; secondary viral or bacterial infections; FIP; respiratory problems; parasitic infections; and arthritis.

Treatment of FeLV involves isolation and management of all the secondary infections, including any cancerous growths that appear. A vaccination exists but will not cure a cat who already has the condition.

A few cats infected with FeLV do not actually become sick, but carry the virus for the rest of their lives. A carrier can be detected through a simple blood test; these cats should be isolated from others for the rest of their lives.

To protect your cat from FeLV, vaccinate her early and keep the vaccinations current; keep the cat indoors; don't bring strays into the home; have any new cat tested for FeLV before bringing him into your home; and avoid boarding your cat.

FELINE PANLEUKOPENIA

Also called distemper or feline infectious enteritis, this dangerous viral condition, prevalent among outdoor and stray cats, is often but not always fatal. A hardy virus, panleukopenia is passed from cat to cat through contact with any bodily secretion. Unlike most other viral contagions, this one can remain a potent source of infection for weeks outside of a host. Even normal disinfecting may not kill it; only cleaning with a dilute bleach solution seems to render it harmless.

Also occurring in raccoons, panleukopenia attacks the host's bone marrow, intestinal lining, and any other quickly replicating cells, causing gastrointestinal damage, anemia, immune-system damage, and secondary infections. Signs of panleukopenia include high fever; lethargy; dehydration; loss of appetite and weight; diarrhea and vomiting; and secondary bacterial and viral infections.

Panleukopenia is a potent killer of kittens. Pregnant females infected during late gestation will often give birth to kittens who have malformations of the cerebellum (cerebellar hypoplasia). Signs become apparent at around three weeks of age; they include a spastic, drunken gait, head tilt, and twitching.

Treatment should begin as quickly as possible, particularly in young cats, because panleukopenia can kill rapidly. Your vet will do a full exam and a blood test to confirm the diagnosis, then begin administering fluids, antibiotics, and sometimes blood transfusions.

Ensure that your cat receives proper vaccinations when young, then take precautions against bringing the virus into your environment. Avoid exposing your cat to any unvaccinated cats, particularly strays; avoid boarding your cat out if possible; and do not let him go outside. Have any new cats checked for panleukopenia before they ever set foot in your home.

FELINE RESPIRATORY DISEASE COMPLEX (FRDC)

Cats get colds and flu just like humans do. Caused by several viral and bacterial agents, these common conditions, though rarely fatal, can make your cat very unhappy. All are contagious, and transmission can be airborne or by physical contact. A cat can develop one or more respiratory diseases in her lifetime, just as we all certainly catch many colds and flu. Though not life-threatening, it's still important to bring your cat to the doctor when she's not feeling well, because colds and flu have many symptoms in common with more serious conditions. You'll probably need to encourage your cat to eat if he's sick with a respiratory infection, because cats often won't eat well if they can't smell their food.

Keep your cat indoors, prevent contact with strays, and avoid boarding facilities to reduce risk of Feline Respiratory Disease Complex.

Caused by a bacterial infection, this is acquired through contact with other cats. Symptoms include discharge from eyes and nose; sneezing; and conjunctivitis. Once your vet properly diagnoses the problem, he'll prescribe antibiotics to kill the infection. If your cat has *Chlamydia psittaci*, keep her away from other cats for at least a month.

Feline Calicivirus (FCV)

There are many different strains of FCV, also known as feline flu, making vaccination difficult. Though not normally life-threatening to the adult cat, it can be dangerous for the young or old. The condition causes a fever that may last for several days. Ulcerations of the mouth can also occur, as can breathing difficulties, sneezing, and discharge. Loss of weight and appetite is possible, as is vomiting, diarrhea, and dehydration. FCV can weaken a cat, allowing secondary infections to take hold.

The cat must rest and take medication to combat infection. Fluids might also need to be administered to keep the cat hydrated. Antidiarrheal medication may be needed as well. Prevent FCV by getting your cat properly vaccinated on a regular basis.

Feline Viral Rhinotracheitis (FVR)

Also referred to simply as "rhino," this condition is caused by herpes virus type one (not related to the herpes virus in humans). A cat with FVR will have cold-like symptoms: sneezing, coughing, and runny eyes and nose. She may have conjunctivitis, fever, and a loss of appetite as well. In rare cases, FVR can be fatal, particularly to newborn kittens. It can last up to ten days; cats who have had it can remain carriers for the rest of their lives. FVR can become dormant as well, popping up during times of stress.

Your vet will prescribe antiviral medication, as well as antibiotics to fight secondary infection. Keeping the cat warm, dry, and hydrated will aid in recovery. Always keep an infected cat away from others. FVR can be prevented through vaccination.

Feline Urologic Syndrome (FUS)

Cats suffering from FUS experience bladder or urethral stones that lead to blockage, urine retention, and infection. A fairly common problem in older cats, symptoms include frequent urination with little result; blood in the urine; excessive licking of the genital area; restlessness and irritability; and a hard, full bladder.

Diagnosed through examination, urine testing, and X-rays, stones blocking the urethral passage can be serious. Urine retention can lead to severe dehydration, kidney damage from built-up toxins, and even death.

Stones that block the urethral passage are formed over time, and are directly related to the cat's diet (though recent studies suggest a genetic component). The food a cat eats affects the composition and pH of his urine; the wrong food can encourage stones. Elements that contribute to stone formation include high levels of magnesium; low water intake, which concentrates urine and encourages crystal formation; infrequent urination; dry-food-only diet; and inferior-quality food. If your cat is having a hard time passing urine, see your vet immediately. The vet can check bladder fullness and determine if a blockage is present.

FUS is more common in males than in females because of the male's thinner, longer urethra; the penis may become slightly extended or bloody at the tip. A urine test will confirm the presence of mineral crystals as well as an alkaline pH, which is conducive to the formation of stones. Your vet may actually be able to remove small, sandy mineral obstructions by simple manipulation if they are located close to the tip of the penis.

Complete urinary obstruction can become life-threatening within 48 hours due to toxin buildup in the blood. Cats who urinate outside are at highest risk, since owners cannot tell when the cat has last relieved himself. Severe cases require urinary catheterization, hospitalization, and fluid therapy to flush the kidneys and detoxify the system.

Treatment may include drugs that acidify the urine. Your vet will also prescribe a food that discourages crystal buildup and a more acidic pH for the urine. You can prevent FUS by using quality food that is not alkali or high in magnesium; supplementing dry food with canned food that has an ample fat content; providing plenty of fresh, clean water; changing litter frequently; and exercising your cat.

GASTRITIS

An inflammation of the stomach lining, gastritis can occur suddenly or become chronic. If left untreated it can create bleeding ulcers. Possible irritants include consumption of toxic plants or drugs, spoiled food, or grass; stomach infection due to bacteria; stress; and sudden change of diet.

Symptoms include vomiting, diarrhea, black feces, anemia, fatigue, restlessness, and irritability.

Gastritis can be indicative of a more serious illness. Your vet will suggest some solutions and preventative measures, such as removing toxic substances, including plants, drugs, cleaning products, and solvents; feeding your cat a good-quality food; wetting dry food before serving it; and minimizing stress.

Cat Tales: Hairball Problems

It used to be that mineral oil would be the recommended treatment for cats who were having trouble with hairballs. Nowadays, however, hairball medications are preferred, as mineral oil can drain nutrients. If vomiting due to hairballs becomes chronic, or if your cat's weight and appetite decrease, see your vet.

If you think your cat is sensitive or allergic to a particular type of food or treat, slowly change over to another brand and see what happens.

HEART DISEASE

The heart is the most important muscle in the cat's body, and when something goes wrong with it or when it has a defect of some sort, a cat's health can be severely compromised.

Except for atherosclerosis (narrowing of the coronary arteries), which is rare in cats, most heart diseases that affect humans can affect cats as well, including congenital defects, infections, tumors, muscle disorders, injury, nutritional deficiencies, poisoning, and arrhythmias. Actual heart attacks are rare in cats; instead, problems occur over a longer period of time, often making diagnosis difficult.

Advanced techniques, such as ECG (electrocardiography), X-rays, coronary angiography, CT scanning, echocardiography, MRI (magnetic resonance imaging), blood tests, biopsy, and coronary catheterization, can be used to investigate and diagnose heart disease in cats.

Congenital Defects

Structural abnormalities of the heart are common in kittens. They include septal defects, or "holes" in the heart as well as defects involving the heart valves. Hereditary factors do not seem to play a great role; when a kitten is afflicted, others in the same litter often have no heart problems at all. Symptoms include breathlessness; pale or bluish pallor to mucous membranes; stunted growth; underdeveloped muscles; and fatigue.

Congenital defects can be diagnosed by X-ray, ECG, or echocardiography. Treatment can include rest, drug therapy, oxygen, and a change in diet.

Infections

Certain viral or bacterial infections can cause damage to the cat's heart and impede function. Endocarditis, an infection of the heart valves, can cause the deformity and malfunction of one or more valves. Diagnosis is normally made through blood tests, X-rays, and ECG. For true endocarditis, treatment involves antibiotics.

Tumors

Though uncommon, heart tumors and cancers do occur inside the heart chambers, in the heart muscle itself, or in the pericardium (the sac surrounding the heart). These can affect heartbeat, and may lead to heart failure.

Diagnosis involves blood tests, ECG, X-rays, and physical examination. Treatment usually depends on the severity and location of the growth; if it is small and benign, quite often it will just be monitored. If the growth is malignant, however, anticancer drug therapy can be administered to slow down or reverse the growth and to prevent its spread. A change in diet, as well as rest, may also be advised.

Muscle Disorders

Cardiomyopathy is a term used for disease of the heart muscle that may be fatal. It can be hereditary, brought on by dietary deficiencies, or caused by poisoning, hyperthyroidism, or viral infection. Myocarditis, the inflammation of the heart muscle, is also caused by a viral or bacterial infection, though some drugs can also cause it. Diagnosis is through ECG, blood tests, and physical examination. Treatment can involve drug therapy, dietary change, and rest.

Cat Tales: More Heart Troubles

Trauma to the chest, nutritional deficiencies, obesity, and poisoning can also damage a cat's heart. Drug therapy, change in diet, rest, and sometimes surgery is required. In the case of poisoning, vomiting often must be induced also, although there are some poisons where it is not good to induce vomiting.

Arrhythmia and Other Disorders

An arrhythmia is a disturbance in the rhythm of the cat's heartbeat. A heart murmur is caused by an irregular turbulence of blood within the heart. Though not always serious, these conditions must be addressed by a vet. A murmur could point to abnormal heart valve function, anemia, or muscle disease. Heart block, a condition involving the improper synchronicity of the upper and lower heart chambers, can cause dizziness, shortness of breath, and death.

Your vet can diagnose these conditions through physical exams and tests; she may want to prescribe drugs to regulate the problem or simply monitor it over time.

Though many forms of heart disease are either hereditary or congenital, you can minimize the occurrence by feeding your cat quality food; preventing obesity; giving your cat enough exercise; storing toxic substances safely out of reach; and keeping your cat indoors to avoid infections or injuries that could bring on heart problems.

Hip Dysplasia

Hip dysplasia is a deformity of the hip joint where the head of the femur fails to fit into the socket of the pelvis. More common in purebred than mixed-breed cats, it can affect one or both hip joints. Hip dysplasia is largely a hereditary phenomenon, which makes it unpreventable. However, many breeders are starting to screen their breeding cats for this condition. Cats with hip dysplasia have a much higher incidence of arthritis and joint pain later in life. They are also vulnerable to injuries due to their joint instability.

To diagnose hip dysplasia your vet will examine your cat and take X-rays. In many cases, the condition will remain stable provided the cat does not become a wild acrobat and stays near her ideal weight. In cases where the cat is in pain or simply cannot walk, your vet may prescribe drugs to relieve the discomfort or possibly opt for surgery.

Hyper- and Hypothyroidism

A condition that causes the overproduction of thyroid hormones, hyperthyroidism is possibly the most common problem of the feline endocrine system. Usually associated with older cats, it can appear in youngsters as well.

Symptoms of hyperthyroidism are numerous, sometimes making it a difficult condition to diagnose. They include enlarged thyroid gland; atrophied muscles; weight loss despite ravenous appetite; restlessness and irritability; bulging eyes; diarrhea, vomiting, and excessive urination; higher blood pressure and heart rate; and possible kidney damage.

Diagnosis is confirmed through physical examination and testing to measure thyroid hormone levels in the blood. Analysis of the cat's urine will determine if kidney damage has been done; chest X-rays will assess whether other organs have been affected.

Treatment calls for drug therapy that will inhibit the production of thyroid hormones, or, in some cases, involves the surgical removal of part or all of the thyroid gland. Alternatively, administering radioactive iodine, which renders the thyroid gland inactive, may be less stressful to an older cat. Once the overactive thyroid gland has been removed or destroyed, the cat may need supplements of thyroid hormone for the rest of her life. (Often, however, the problem is only on one side of the thyroid gland.)

Hypothyroidism, extremely rare in cats, results when the thyroid gland does not produce enough hormones. Often, the animal becomes unpredictably aggressive, shy, and uneasy, and he may develop abnormal skin and coat problems. This condition can be diagnosed through a blood test to measure hormone levels. Once hypothyroidism is confirmed, hormone supplementation can bring the cat back to normal behavioral and physical health.

Although it's not totally established, veterinarians believe that there is probably a genetic predisposition involved in both conditions. Infection, inflammation, and possibly diet (including high iodine levels in food) could cause these problems as well. There's not much you can do to prevent them, short of feeding a good-quality food and maintaining your cat's general health.

INCONTINENCE

Defined as uncontrolled involuntary urination, incontinence can result from numerous causes, including injury or disease of the urinary tract. This disorder often affects older cats, partly because the efficiency of the sphincter muscles surrounding the urethra declines with age. Incontinence can also be caused by abnormal stress in the cat's environment.

Infections, stones, and tumors can all cause your cat to become incontinent, as can damage to the brain or spinal cord. Trauma to the pelvic area or even cystitis can also bring on this condition.

If you suspect that your cat is incontinent (and not just house soiling or marking), see your vet immediately. He will test the cat's urine to determine if there is infection, inflammation, diabetes, or stone formation present. Ultrasound and X-rays can be done to determine if there is an obstruction. Physical examination can help to tell if the cat's bladder or urethra is damaged or infected; a constantly full bladder can point to FUS, and must be dealt with.

Feeding a quality, vet-approved food, maintaining the cat's general health, and keeping him out of stressful situations can help.

INTESTINAL DISORDERS

The cat's intestinal system is sometimes subject to structural abnormalities and the effects of many infectious organisms. It can also be affected by tumors, blockages, improper blood supply, and other disorders.

Congenital Defects

Kittens are sometimes born with intestinal blockages. Looping of the bowel, narrowing of the small intestine, the absence of an anal opening, or blockage due to fetal intestinal contents (meconium) can all occur. Surgery is often not possible with kittens; the procedure (especially the anesthesia) can be too traumatic to the newborn. Adult cats can survive intestinal surgery, however, with no real problems.

Infections

Viral or bacterial agents can attack the intestines, causing minor to life-threatening problems. Protozoans (such as *Toxoplasma* and *Giardia*) can cause diarrhea and symptoms similar to those of gastritis. Worms and intestinal ulcerations are possible sources of infection. Drug therapy and change of diet are the typical courses of treatment.

Tumors

Tumors are more common in the large intestine, although they do sometimes occur in the small intestine as well. If malignant, these can spread through the body, causing secondary malignancies. Treatment includes anticancer drugs, surgery, and dietary change.

Impaired Blood Supply

Lack of sufficient blood supply, caused by an obstruction of arteries in the abdominal wall, compression of blood vessels from a hernia, or even injury, can cause tissue death requiring corrective surgery.

Obstructions

Tumors, stones, or constipation can all lead to intestinal blockages, as can ingestion of "foreign" objects like the thread of Christmas tree tinsel. (So steer clear of tinsel during the holidays!) Treatment can involve drug therapy, surgery, and dietary change. Though ulcers of the intestinal tract are rare, cats can develop them as a result of improper diet, stress, or viral infection. Treatment involves drug therapy and dietary change.

The problem can be diagnosed through physical exam, as well as barium X-rays, sigmoidoscopy, or colonoscopy (viewing scopes inserted into the intestines); lab examination of feces; or biopsy of a specimen of intestinal lining.

Prevent feline intestinal disorders by feeding your cat quality food; seeing to his general health; keeping him indoors; and visiting the vet once per year.

KIDNEY DISEASE

The kidneys filter blood and excrete waste products and excess water in the form of urine. Without proper kidney function, toxins overwhelm the body, leading to coma and death. Symptoms of kidney disease include increased thirst and/or urination; loss of appetite and weight; incontinence and vomiting; bad breath; diabetes; and high blood pressure.

Congenital Disorders

Cats are sometimes born with deformed kidneys, or with only one, reducing filtering capacity by half. Cats can also inherit a cystic disorder that can impair kidney function.

Impaired Blood Supply

Diabetes can decrease the supply of blood to the kidneys, resulting in tissue damage. Blockages to the renal arteries can also damage the kidneys. Surgery, drug therapy, and dietary change can help to correct these problems.

Metabolic Disorders

Kidney stones, caused by high concentrations of various types of minerals in the blood, can be painful and damaging to kidney function. Surgery, dietary change, and drug therapy can help reduce their formation.

Infections

The cat's kidneys can become infected if a bladder infection, caused by a blockage of the urethra, goes untreated. Stagnant, bacteria-laden urine can spread an infection up from the bladder to the kidneys. The blockage can be caused by a stone, congenital defect, tumor, or injury to the urethra. Treatment of this type of condition involves removal of the blockage, drug therapy, and dietary change.

Toxic Substances

A number of toxic substances can damage a cat's kidneys, most commonly antifreeze. This damage can be irreversible, so it is vital to keep your cat away from toxic substances.

Tumors

Though rare, cats can develop kidney tumors. As tumors can seriously affect kidney function, early detection and surgical removal, combined with drug therapy and dietary change, are necessary.

Detecting problems with your cat's kidneys is not easy. Pay close attention to your cat's everyday health, and visit the vet at the first sign of trouble. Sadly, in some cases, kidney disease can be fatal, especially when the problem is congenital. Nevertheless, if caught early, kidney disease can often be arrested, extending the cat's life. These days, cats are leaders in kidney transplants, and families are required to adopt the donor cats.

Minimize the chances of kidney disease by feeding your cat a diet that is not excessively high in salt, phosphorus, and protein and supplying plenty of clean, fresh water each day.

LIVER DISEASE

The liver is one of the body's most important organs. Regulating the levels of most of the chemicals in the blood, it also produces proteins for the blood plasma, helps to regulate the distribution of fats in the body, and stores glycogen, which is used as an energy source when needed. In addition, the liver regulates amino acid levels and helps clear the blood of certain toxins. A resilient organ, the liver can partially regenerate, and it will continue to function even after over half of it has been removed.

Liver disease is not uncommon, particularly among older cats. It is a serious matter, because without the liver, life is not possible. Symptoms include diarrhea and vomiting; weight and appetite loss; lethargy and irritability; jaundice; and epilepsy.

Congenital Defects

Malformed bile ducts can affect liver function. There are few other congenital defects.

Infections

Bacterial or viral infections, generally known as hepatitis, can seriously affect liver function. Parasites, too, can cause disease; flukes, a type of worm, can be injurious to the liver.

Treatment involves drug therapy and dietary change, as well as limiting your cat's contact with other infectious animals.

Poisoning

Many drugs and toxins can injure your cat's liver. As explained earlier in this chapter, aspirin can sometimes be used safely with cats, but only at very low dosages and at long dosing intervals. Acetaminophen, ibuprofen, alcohol, insecticides, and solvents should all be avoided, as should toxic plants, particularly wild mushrooms.

Tumors

Cancerous tumors can spread to a cat's liver from other areas of the body. Tumors can develop independently on the liver, though this is rare. Treatment includes surgery, drug therapy, and dietary change.

You can help lessen the chances of liver disease by keeping your cat indoors, away from bacterial, viral, and parasitic infection, feeding him a vet-approved diet; and steering clear of any toxic materials.

OBESITY

One of the most common disorders in domestic cats, obesity is often brought on by overfeeding and lack of activity—a problem increasingly common among cats, dogs, *and* humans. Simply put, any animal gains weight when caloric intake exceeds energy output. Generally, if a cat (or person) is more than 15 to 20 percent over his ideal body weight, he's probably obese. A healthy domestic cat should usually not weigh more than 12 to 14 pounds, unless he is a large breed, such as a Maine coon or Norwegian forest cat. So, if you have a 23-pounder waddling around, you have a problem.

Obesity is hard on a cat. It puts needless stress on the heart, lungs, joints, and muscles, and will result in lethargy and inactivity. Obesity also opens a cat up to a variety of disorders, including diabetes, liver, and heart problems.

Occasionally, obesity can be brought on by a medical problem such as hypothyroidism (an underactive thyroid gland). Neutering and aging can also slow a cat's metabolism down somewhat. If your cat is gaining too much weight, you should either reduce her food intake accordingly or change to a low-calorie "senior" food. To prevent obesity in your kitty, remember to feed her at regular intervals, limit treats and begging, and encourage plenty of exercise (see Chapter 7).

OTITIS EXTERNA

A common inflammation of the outer ear, otitis externa can be caused by ear mites, but it's usually caused by infection. Bacteria or fungi can infect the entire canal and even the external ear itself, sometimes resulting in a skin disorder akin to dermatitis.

A cat suffering from this condition will have wax buildup or even pus in the affected ear, and will incessantly shake and scratch the ear in an effort to relieve discomfort. The inside of the ear can appear inflamed and red, and may have a bad odor. Head straight to the vet for proper diagnosis and care, because if left untreated, infection can spread to the middle and inner ear, causing permanent damage. Your vet will inspect the cat's ear, clean it out with disinfectant solution, and treat with antibiotics. You'll probably have to continue the cleaning at home. The vet may even provide medicated ointment; use it until directed otherwise. Ask your vet to recommend an ear cleaner for regular use at home when needed.

You can lessen the chances of your cat's developing otitis externa by regularly cleaning his ears and preventing infestations of ear mites. Keeping the cat indoors will cut the chances of any infections taking hold.

PNEUMONIA

A serious inflammation of the lungs caused by infection, pneumonia is most often a complication of another illness such as feline immunodeficiency virus. Caused by a virus, bacterium, protozoan, or fungus, pneumonia generally results in fever, shortness of breath, sneezing and wheezing, plus a bad cough that produces a yellow-green sputum, sometimes mixed with blood. Pneumonia is far more common in older cats and very young kittens than in healthy adults.

Your vet can diagnose pneumonia by listening to your cat's chest with a stethoscope, taking X-rays, and examining the sputum. Treatment depends on the organism causing the infection, and can include antibiotics or other drug therapy. Rest is imperative; any activity that places strain on the lungs should be avoided. Confining the sick cat to one room might be advisable, provided the room is warm and free of drafts. Total recovery can take six to eight weeks; don't let the cat have contact with other animals during this time.

You can reduce the chances of your cat contracting pneumonia by keeping him indoors, and away from other sick cats. Keep kittens and old cats warm and dry.

RABIES

An acute viral infection of the nervous system, rabies is also known as hydrophobia. Transmitted by a bite or a lick on an open sore, the virus travels from the wound along the nerve pathways to the brain, where it causes inflammation and infection that leads to spasms, pain, delirium, paralysis, and bizarre behavior. Once infected with rabies, a cat almost always dies. Bats, skunks, raccoons, and foxes are all known carriers and can infect your cat, which is why it is so important to vaccinate your cat by four months of age and always keep boosters current throughout your cat's life.

RICKETS

A nutritional deficiency disease that affects the skeleton of the growing kitten, rickets is characterized by inadequate incorporation of calcium and phosphate into the bones. The most common cause is a lack of dietary vitamin D, which is needed for calcium absorption. Any good-quality cat food should have sufficient quantities of all needed vitamins and minerals, so just double check to make sure that the food you feed has adequate amounts of vitamin D.

RINGWORM

Deceptively named, ringworm is a fairly common contagious fungal infection of the skin, nails, or hair, spread through contact with another infected animal or through contact with airborne fungal spores. More common in younger cats and sickly adults, ringworm can take hold while a cat is suffering from a serious disorder or is under great stress. Ringworm is transmissible to humans.

Symptoms include loss of coat in circular patches, scaly areas, and deformed nails. Ringworm can be hard to diagnose because symptoms can be similar to dermatitis or mite infestation. Cats can also be asymptomatic carriers. Your vet will need to examine a scraping of affected skin or grow a culture to confirm the diagnosis. Topical solutions will be applied to the affected areas after they have been shaved. You might need to continue the treatments at home for several days. Oral medications are sometimes used in severe cases. All animals in the home will need to receive at least a medicated bath, even if they show no overt signs.

Prevention includes thoroughly cleaning your home to rid it of any ringworm spores that might be present. Keeping your cat indoors and away from outdoor cats will also help. There is a vaccine for ringworm now, but it's generally only used in cattery situations.

STOMACH DISORDERS

Stomach disorders are fairly common, and can occur due to the following.

Infections

Though normally protected from infection by the strong acidic secretions present, the cat's stomach can suffer when this protection fails for some reason. Stomach ulcers, though rare in cats, can occur when the stomach's protective mucous lining breaks down, allowing acid to destroy stomach tissue. Certain viruses are perhaps thought to cause this situation; they attack and destroy the mucous membranes, allowing the acid to digest stomach tissues.

Tumors

Stomach cancer, also uncommon in cats, can occur as metastasized tumors spread from other areas or as primary tumors originating in the stomach. Causes can be hereditary, dietary, or related to environment. Symptoms include loss of weight and appetite, and vomiting.

Treatment for stomach cancer can include surgery, anticancer drugs, and dietary change.

Stomach disorders can be investigated through barium X-ray exams or gastroscopy, the examination of the stomach by a flexible viewing tube. A biopsy of stomach tissue might also be performed.

Help minimize stomach disorders by feeding your cat good-quality food, and by keeping her indoors, away from other cats carrying viruses or harmful bacteria. Avoid feeding your cat rich foods or anything meant for human consumption.

TETANUS

A serious, often fatal disease of the central nervous system, tetanus is caused by infection of a wound with spores from the bacteria *Clostridium tetani*. Cats seem to be more resistant to this bacteria than humans; because of this, vaccination for it is rare. The offending bacteria can be found in soil, feces, and almost anywhere else.

Symptoms include stiffness throughout the body (including "lockjaw"), fever, restlessness, and problems with breathing or swallowing. Your vet can diagnose this condition and treat your cat with antibiotics. Keeping your cat indoors can minimize the chance of your cat contracting tetanus.

ULCERS

An open sore on the skin or on a mucous membrane (such as the gums or the lining of the stomach), ulcers destroy tissue, and usually become inflamed and painful. Skin ulcers on a cat are common, and can result from allergic or contact dermatitis or from parasitic infection. Treatment involves administering oral or topical drugs.

Ulcers of the mucous membranes usually occur in the digestive tract or mouth, and can be caused by viral infection, food allergy, parasitic infestation, or ingestion of a toxic substance. Treatment involves drug therapy, change of diet, and, rarely, surgery.

Minimize the chance of ulcers by ensuring your cat is parasite-free, eats quality food, and is kept away from any potential allergic substances.

URETHRITIS

Defined as the inflammation of the cat's urethra, urethritis is frequently caused by an infection but can have other causes, such as trauma or chemical irritants. A cat suffering from this condition will feel pain and may have great difficulty passing urine. This can lead to a bladder infection and the formation of stones. Treatment usually calls for antibiotics to cure the infection. A change of diet may also be advised. Keeping your cat indoors can help prevent this problem.

VOMITING

Vomiting can be a symptom of serious illness in a cat. It can be caused by worm infestation; food poisoning; ulcers, cancer, or diabetes; kidney or liver damage; gastrointestinal disease; serious viral disorders; hairballs; and even stress. Vomiting can also be a harmless reaction to eating grass or rancid meat. Although normally not a cause for great alarm, when an otherwise healthy cat vomits excessively, it can lead to malnourishment and dehydration. If vomiting persists, consult your vet.

If your cat vomits but seems otherwise healthy, try feeding her smaller meals; soaking dry food in water before serving; and preventing her from chewing on or ingesting houseplants or any other toxic substance. If your cat vomits only after eating a certain type of food, eliminate this food from the cat's diet and see what happens. You should also groom your cat more frequently to discourage hairball development.

If there are any other animals in the home (especially another cat), consider quarantining the vomiting cat until the cause is found.

YEAST INFECTIONS

Commonly found in conjunction with cases of feline ear infections (see Otitis Externa), a yeast infection can cause buildup of a dark brown waxy discharge as well as an unpleasant smell. The cat may shake his head and scratch due to the discomfort. Your vet can easily correct the problem by liberally cleaning out your cat's ears. You may be able to prevent yeast infections by cleaning your cat's ears regularly with equal parts of water and white vinegar, then applying a commercially available ear powder to keep things dry. If in doubt, to the vet you must go!

Appendix

Cat Associations and Organizations

Local animal shelters, breeders, and breed clubs are too numerous to list here. Contact any of the organizations below for information about resources in your area.

American Cat Fancier Association

P.O. Box 1949
Nixa, MO 65714-1949
(417) 725-1530
www.acfacat.com

American Society for the Prevention of Cruelty to Animals (ASPCA)

424 East 92nd Street
New York, NY 10128-6804
(212) 876-7700
www.aspca.org

Best Friends Animal Society and Sanctuary

5001 Angel Canyon Rd.
Kanab, UT 84741-5000
(435) 644-2001
www.bestfriends.org

Canadian Cat Association

289 Rutherford Rd. S. #18
Brampton, Ontario
Canada L6W 3R9
(905) 459-1481
www.cca-afc.com

Cat Fanciers' Association

P.O. Box 1005
Manasquan, NJ 08736-0805
(732) 528-9797
www.cfainc.org

Cat Fancier's Federation

P.O. Box 661
Gratis, OH 45330
(973) 787-9009
www.cffinc.org

The Humane Society of the United States

2100 L Street, NW
Washington, DC 20037
(202) 452-1100
www.hsus.org

Printed in the United States
By Bookmasters